Writing a Research Paper in Political Science

A Practical Guide to Inquiry, Structure, and Methods

LISA A. BAGLIONE
Saint Joseph's University

THOMSON

WADSWORTH

Australia • Brazil • Canada • Mexico • Singapore
Spain • United Kingdom • United States

To Steve

THOMSON
WADSWORTH

Writing a Research Paper in Political Science:
A Practical Guide to Inquiry, Structure, and Methods
Lisa A. Baglione

Executive Editor: David Tatom
Associate Development Editor:
  Rebecca Green
Editorial Assistant: Eva Dickerson
Technology Project Manager:
  Michelle Vardeman
Senior Marketing Manager: Janise Fry
Marketing Assistant: Teresa Jessen
Marketing Communications Manager:
  Nathaniel Bergson-Michelson
Senior Project Manager, Editorial
  Production: Paul Wells

Creative Director: Rob Hugel
Art Director: Maria Epes
Print Buyer: Judy Inouye
Permissions Editor: Kiely Sisk
Production Service: International
  Typesetting and Composition
Copy Editor: Cheryl S. Smith
Cover Designer: Garry Harman
Compositor: International Typesetting
  and Composition
Printer: Transcontinental Printing/
  Louisville

Printed in Canada
  2 3 4 5 6 7 10 09 08 07 06

Library of Congress Control Number:
2006922147

ISBN 13: 978-0-495-09262-9
ISBN 10: 0-495-09262-2

Thomson Higher Education
10 Davis Drive
Belmont, CA 94002-3098
USA

Brief Contents

Contents

Preface

The purpose of this book is to fill a major void in the literature on research and writing in Political Science. While there are numerous high-quality texts on Research Methods (and far more general social science methodology books) as well as a number of excellent writing style guides, there are no works that are explicitly designed to help students write a research paper, from start to finish. In filling this gap, this work seeks to accomplish some of what both of the other kinds of books do—provide students with an understanding and appreciation for the logic of inquiry and social science methodology and further develop written communication skills—but it also does more. Its aims are to teach students what a research paper contains and how to write one well. To achieve these goals, this book has to teach research, methodological, logical, analytic, and writing skills. Perhaps no other texts currently do this because accomplishing these tasks is seemingly so difficult. Or perhaps the absence of similar books reflects the faculty's deep internalization of the norms and conventions of research-paper writing.[1] We know them and have known them for so long that the process almost seems natural, one innate to everyone. But as all of us who grade student research papers bemoan, a wide proportion of our students clearly lack the skill set required to write an excellent one.

---

[1]Thomas Deans, *Writing and Community Action: A Service-Learning Rhetoric with Readings* (New York: Longman, 2003), p. 136.

If someone had told me when I started teaching that I would be writing this book, I would have been incredulous. Interestingly, my first significant teaching job had me mentoring about ten students a semester who were writing public policy theses at Cornell University's Washington Center. That experience was invaluable for my development as a Political Scientist and as a teacher. I am sure that many of the ideas that are central to this book were planted by Jack Moran and Steve Jackson, the two intellectual forces behind the Cornell-in-Washington program. Jack originally developed an approach to teaching research methods that broke the process down and focused on writing each piece of the paper. Thus, Cornell students wrote a Literature Review, developed a model and argument, designed their research project, and then performed their data analysis. When I was at the Cornell Center, Steve was teaching the course in this same way. Obviously, I have taken this idea but developed it further. In addition to arriving at my own approaches to explaining these sections of a research paper, I have added detailed discussions on arriving at a question, writing an introduction, coming up with good headings and titles, presenting an effective conclusion, and editing and revising.

My interest in and desire to pursue this project has evolved as my academic career has. In many ways, it has developed in response to the huge student need for help in improving writing and research skills. I have learned that students who can write good, even excellent essays are at a loss when they need to complete a major research paper. I shouldn't have been surprised, because this kind of writing is by no means "natural" and is not something that is taught in secondary school or even at the college level. Thus, my own experience has made me realize that a book that teaches how to write a research paper is vitally necessary for college students.

In addition, I have been teaching a course on research paper writing and have been encouraged by colleagues to put my ideas forth in book form. My hesitation to pursue such a project stems from my recognition that what I have to say is not news to any professional political scientist. It is common sense for someone with a Ph.D. But I owe an enormous debt of gratitude to Francis Graham Lee, especially, for convincing me that while these basic ideas are not necessarily groundbreaking, no one has put them forward in book form in this way and no one has found a way to summarize and simplify the elements of the research paper as I have. Graham and I have team-taught a course on basic methodology and writing skills in one form or another for the last ten years at Saint Joseph's University. He has been a wonderful sounding board for my ideas, and with his help,

I have pursued this project. Moreover, I know that I have included many of his ideas here (the Introduction as a "contract," the Introduction as a "first impression," and the importance of feeling proud of one's final paper, to name a few). I was also very lucky that Kevin Wardlaw, who was then the book representative from Wadsworth/Thomson, happened to drop into my office on the day of one of these conversations with Graham and greeted the idea of this book very enthusiastically. I thank Kevin for helping to convince his editor David Tatom that this book was worth publishing. David has also been extremely helpful and patient. I am very grateful for his forbearance and support. And Eva Dickerson, his assistant, has handled my work with great care. The Thomson team also did a fantastic job finding me three wonderful reviewers. I gratefully acknowledge the advice and comments of Scott Robinson and Robert Ostergard, and I'd like to give special thanks to Michael Kanner. The efforts of these three reviewers have certainly improved the final text. In addition, I would like to thank the copy editor, Cheryl S. Smith, the patient and highly competent staff at ITC, Ben Kolstad and Mona Tiwary, and Robert Swanson, my indexer.

Other faculty colleagues, both at SJU and elsewhere, have also been enormously important. I never would have written this book if Ronald Libby hadn't insisted that SJU's Political Science Department institute a Methods course and asserted that I was the one to teach it. As I was writing, I received an enormous amount of encouragement and enthusiasm from colleagues at Saint Joseph's and elsewhere, especially Susan Liebell, Graham Lee, Steve McGovern, Wes Widmaier, Jack Moran, Susanna Wing, and Marissa Golden. Susan, Graham, Steve, and Wes all pored over this text and provided me with helpful comments. Susan, in particular, has spent hours talking to me about this project, and I have received numerous ideas as well as well-timed support from her. Jack, Susanna, and Marissa were always interested in my progress on this project and repeatedly acknowledged that they were interested in the final product. Perhaps most proudly (and humbly), I thankfully acknowledge the guidance that I received from a former student, now Ph.D., Mary Frances Malone. I am so proud to be able to say that I was one of her teachers and humbled to have had one of my former students give me such excellent advice on how to communicate and explain more effectively the elements of the research design and data analysis. I also want to thank George Dowdall, Kim Logio, and Deborah Lurie, again all from SJU, for reminding me of some techniques of data analysis that I had long forgotten.

Of course, my students at Saint Joseph's University contributed enormously to the creation and content of this book. This text is a direct product of my many attempts at explaining to them how to write a research paper. While they do not always appreciate learning the skills associated with that task, most students conclude at some point during the course (or thereafter) that learning to write a political science research paper is important. A few students – Erika Rendeiro, Matt Duncan, Diana Silva, and another who wishes to remain anonymous – allowed me to use their work as examples in this text. I am extremely grateful for their generosity. Two others, Shruti Mehta and Kristen Greenbaum, helped put my bibliography in proper shape. At various points in this process, Jane Frangiosa, the Administrative Assistant for the SJU Political Science Department, also lent a hand. Despite all this wonderful help and inspiration, I alone am responsible for any flaws that remain in the text.

I dedicate this book to my husband, Steve McGovern, who has (among other things) helped me develop as a political scientist, researcher, and writer over the last fifteen years. Without him, I would have given up on academia long ago, but his confidence in me and his ability to teach me how to write better, evaluate arguments with evidence, and think more clearly have helped keep me in this profession which I so dearly love. His optimism about me and about life is a wonderful gift that I cherish. I thank him for his love, support, and partnership on which I can count as a constant, even when I am grading research papers!

About the Author

Dr. Lisa A. Baglione   is an Associate Professor of Political Science and the Director of the International Relations Program at Saint Joseph's University. Her major fields of study are International Relations and Comparative Politics. Dr. Baglione has published works exploring the arms control decision-making process in the United States, the Soviet Union, and Russia, and has coauthored articles on the transformation of the Russian polity and economy in the early post-communist period. Currently, she is researching conflict transformation in the post-Cold War era. At Saint Joseph's, Dr. Baglione teaches a course called Introduction to Political Science Research, in which she developed the ideas, advice, and techniques offered in this work.

1

So, You Have to Write a Research Paper

L et's be honest. When students get a new course syllabus and view the assignments, seeing that the professor has assigned a research paper typically brings one of two reactions. A first possible response is one of horror. Many students dread the assignment because they don't know *how* to write a research paper. Students with this viewpoint may drop the course because of this requirement, be panicked about it all semester, or just ignore the assignment until the last moment (as if it might somehow go away) and then turn "something" in. The other typical response is "No problem, I'll just write a *report* on something I'm interested in." Neither reaction is productive, and the strategies mentioned for dealing with the dreaded assignment are unfortunate for many reasons. The goal of this book is to teach you how to write a research paper so that you (a) won't respond in this fashion and (b) will realize why the typical reactions are so unfortunate.

First, a research paper can be intimidating because—and this point is very important to remember—few secondary schools and institutions of higher learning bother to *teach* how to write one anymore. Yet many faculty give research paper assignments, as if knowing how to write one was an innate ability that all college students possess. Research paper writing, however, is a set of skills that needs to be developed. These skills *can* be taught and learned, and used through-out a college career.

Second, research paper writing is so daunting because the task seems so huge and unbounded. Where do you start? What is a good topic? How do you know where to look for information? What does the text look like in such a paper? How do you know when you're done? This concern with boundaries is obviously related to the general ignorance about what constitutes a research paper. But another problem here is recognizing that writing, whether for a research paper or in some other form, is discipline specific.[1] Faculty often forget to make that point explicitly, and students are used to focusing on writing skills as consisting only of grammar, usage, and paragraph construction. While those skills are certainly important, they are not the only ones that students need to develop for writing a good research paper, particularly in Political Science. Political Science has its own conventions (which are similar to those of the other social sciences and in some instances even related to those in the natural sciences) for paper writing that students must learn. Just because you received an "A" in Freshman English does not mean that you are ready to write and receive an "A" on your Political Science research paper. You must not only learn to speak a new language (the vocabulary of Political Science), but you must adopt the conventions, values, and norms of the discipline.[2] Here again, faculty have so successfully internalized these norms that they forget that students need to be taught them. This book, however, will teach you to

---

[1] For an excellent discussion on the peculiarity of the writing for each field, see Chapter 4 "Writing in Academic Communities" in Thomas Deans, *Writing and Community Action: A Service-Learning Rhetoric with Readings* (New York: Longman, 2003). Deans advances the concept of a "discourse community"—"a group of people who are unified by similar patterns of language use, shared assumptions, common knowledge, and parallel habits of interpretation." Such a term certainly applies to academic disciplines such as Political Science. See p. 136.

[2] *Ibid.* Throughout this chapter, Deans develops the metaphor of writing in a particular discipline as being a traveler, a visitor to "strange lands." He does so by including two interesting works: an essay by Nancy Sakamoto and an article by Lucille McCarthy. Sakamoto examines the differences in the ways Japanese and Americans conceive of and carry on conversations, while McCarthy explicitly uses the phrase "Stranger in Strange Lands" in the title of her paper examining how one particular student fared when trying to write across the curriculum during his freshman and sophomore years.

write a research paper in Political Science, demystifying the structure and the process. Developing this set of writing skills will be useful to you in a number of ways: it will not only help you write more effectively in this discipline, but will allow you to see more easily the conventions that apply to other fields of study. In addition, once you know the style and format for any subject, your reading comprehension skills in that discipline improve and understanding even the densest academic tome becomes easier. Why? Because scholars use this structure themselves, and once you know what to expect from the form of an article or book, you will be more able to distinguish the argument from the evidence, the logic from the information, or the normative claim from the underlying principles.

Third, knowing how to write a research paper is something that will be useful to you throughout your life. You might find that statement funny, thinking to yourself that you are only writing research papers to get your degree, but thereafter, you intend to be working in the corporate or nonprofit world. (My apologies to those of you out there who see an academic career in your future.) Well, if you were amused, you need to stop laughing and recognize that you likely will spend much of your career writing, and a good portion of that writing will be persuasive communication that (a) surveys a number of different opinions or studies on a particular problem, (b) assesses logically the strengths and weaknesses of the various approaches, and (c) uses evidence from a case or cases of particular interest to you, your boss, and/or your clients to determine what the "best" approach to this problem is for your purposes. In effect, then, you are going to be writing research papers for your living, no matter what you do. So, why not learn how to do it now, and develop the aptitude so that you will be in a better position in your future?

Knowing how to write a research paper is an acquired talent, not something that you are born knowing how to do. When you master the set of skills involved, you are empowered. By learning how to write that research paper, you acquire expertise—skills of reading comprehension, writing, research, and analysis—that will enable you to do well in all of your classes. Moreover, these are all talents that you will use in your future career, whether you are an attorney,

CEO, activist, public servant, politician, businessperson, or educator. Such professionals are frequently asked to evaluate information and provide recommendations. For instance, imagine you are working at the United States Justice Department and are asked to determine the impact of the Patriot Act. At the outset, you are going to need to find the legislation itself and then define what "impact" means. You will also need to justify your definition and explain where and why you select the information that you do. Once you have some data, you have to analyze it, and then write up your findings in a form that will impress your boss. You will learn all of the skills required to do an excellent job on this project in this book.

WHAT IS A RESEARCH PAPER? A FEW HELPFUL METAPHORS

Most students think that a research paper in Political Science is a long, descriptive report of some event, phenomenon, or person. This is a dangerous misconception that focuses on determining facts. Numerous methodology and philosophy of science texts will explain that "true facts" are often elusive because researchers interpret what they see or because they report only what they deem important, knowingly or unknowingly, failing to provide a more complete picture.[3] While we will return to the topic of data collection later in the text, the problem that I am raising here is the one that characterizes so many papers: conceiving of them as "data dumps," or all the information that you can find on a particular topic. Descriptive reporting is only one part of a Political Science research paper. It is an important part, and having a chance to learn about politically relevant events,

---

[3]Some works will question whether any "true facts" actually exist. See for example Paul Rabinow and William M. Sullivan, eds., *Interpretive Social Science: A Reader* (Berkeley: University of California Press, 1979). Post-modernists will be disappointed with my discussion of the research process because much of what I ask students to do will seem consistent with "brute data approaches." For that terminology, see Charles Taylor's piece in that book, entitled "Interpretation and the Sciences of Man," on pp. 25–71, especially pp. 53–54. I would argue, however, that the process of how intersubjective understandings come about can be modeled, that we need ways of putting forth contentions about social reality that are systematic, and that one's conclusions can be evaluated by others. Thus, I ask those of you who are skeptical of social scientific methodology because of its inattention to constitutive processes to bear with me to see whether I am able to deliver a guide that works for the kinds of studies that you would like to see performed.

persons or phenomena is probably why you are a Political Science major. But knowing about politics is not being a political scientist. For political scientists, details are important, but only if they are the "right" ones, related to either the logics or norms that you are exploring or the precise evidence that you need to sustain or undermine an argument. Facts for the sake of facts are boring and distracting.

Two different metaphors help to understand the balance that you should seek. The first is that of a court case. In writing your research paper, you are, in essence, presenting your case to the judge and jury (readers of the paper). While you need to acknowledge that there are other possible explanations (for instance, your opposing counsel's case), your job is to show that both your preferred logic and the evidence supporting it are stronger than any competing perspective's framework and its sustaining information. Interesting details that have nothing to do with the particular argument you are constructing can distract a jury and annoy the judge. Good lawyers lay out their cases, connecting all the dots and leaving no pieces of evidence hanging. All the information that they provide is related to convincing those in judgment that their interpretation is the correct one.

If you find the analogy of the courtroom too adversarial, think of your paper as a painting. The level and extent of the detail depends on both the size of the canvas and the subject to be painted. Too few details in a landscape can make it boring and unidentifiable, whereas too many in a portrait can make the subject unattractive or strange.[4]

One more metaphor on which I will rely throughout this book is the research paper as marathon. In both cases, the final product—the paper or the race—is the culmination of great efforts. Just as the typical person cannot expect to get up on the morning of a marathon, go to the starting line, run for more than 26 miles and finish the race, so too, a student needs to go through preparatory steps before completing the research paper. While runners stretch, train, get the right nutrition and rest, and prepare mentally for years, months, and days before the big race, students need to practice their writing and develop their logic, find the "right" kinds of information, and work on stating their case as strongly and effectively as possible. All of these tasks require time and energy. Only with adequate preparation do the marathoner and the student finish the race and the paper, respectively.

While few of us are likely to run a marathon, everyone who reads this book will write a research paper. My point in writing is to show

---

[4]Of course, some artists have had great success with these extremes that I am calling inadequate. Yes, I am a political scientist and not an art critic.

you that if you follow the advice spelled out here, you will not only finish your paper but you will turn in something of which you feel proud. Too often I have seen students rushing at the end just to get their papers done, without really caring about quality. Their feelings are at times understandable. They didn't know how to approach the project, haven't asked for or received any guidance, and are having a totally unsatisfying time working on their research paper. When this is the case, not only is the end result poor, but the exercise itself is a failure as an assignment. You can have a rewarding and satisfying learning experience if you *devote time to the process* and you *conceive of it as consisting of smaller, definable tasks*. Each piece can be accomplished on its own and the parts can then be assembled and reworked to create a coherent and significant whole. In effect, then, the tasks are like the marathoner's efforts to train months and weeks before a race—stretching, running for distance, weight training, getting adequate nutrition and rest—it's then all put together on race day to finish with a respectable time (as each runner defines it).

In fact, if we continue this running analogy, I am asking you to consider the story of the Tortoise and the Hare. I admonish you to be the Tortoise. Slow and steady will win this race. While some people have natural talent (whether it is as runners or writers), individuals finish marathons and write research papers because they are determined, diligent, and skilled. The Hare may be the more naturally gifted and the faster runner, but the Tortoise industriously persists throughout the course to win the race. Be the Tortoise![5] Work on your paper slowly but surely throughout your course, and you will produce a fine final product.

WHAT RESEARCH PAPER
WRITING ENTAILS

This book seeks to teach you the basics of writing a research paper in Political Science. Each chapter is devoted to a particular section of the research paper and the skills that you need to develop in order to make that piece of your final product a good one. The research

---

[5]In working on this book, I learned that Eviatar Zerubavel, in his well-respected work, also uses Aesop's famous fable to explain the approach one should take to writing. See his *The Clockwork Muse: A Practical Guide to Writing Theses, Dissertations, and Books* (Cambridge, MA: Harvard UP, 1999), p. 12.

TABLE 1.1 Research Paper: Tasks to Be Accomplished, Sections (Outline), and Suggested Calendar

Tasks	Sections	*Suggested* Calendar
Finding a "good" topic or, more accurately, a good **research question.**	Introduction	By end of first half of course
Identifying, classifying, and **explaining** the most important **scholarly answers** to that question.	Literature Review Model and Hypothesis	By end of first third of course
Evaluating the appropriateness of one or more of these **answers** for a set of cases that is of particular interest to you.	Research Design Analysis and Assessment	During the second two-thirds of course
Providing a conclusion that reminds the reader of what you found. It also explains why your findings turned out the way they did and suggests further paths for research.	Conclusion	In the last two weeks
Revising and **Editing.**	All sections	Throughout course, but an intense effort in last week

paper writing process can be broken down into five distinct but interrelated tasks,[6] which map into different sections of the paper as specified in Table 1.1. Because institutions use different-length terms (semesters, trimesters, and quarters) and some students using this book might even be writing theses of longer duration, I'm providing a *suggested* calendar in relative terms. By setting out deadlines along the way, I am underlining the notion that you cannot write a research paper in a matter of days or hours. The timing here, however, is *provisional,* and you should look to your instructor's guidelines as you work on your research.

Each of the following chapters will identify precisely what you need to do to accomplish these tasks and write the different sections of the paper. In the text that follows you will find instructions,

---

[6]In their first presentation, these tasks are put forth in a simplified manner. I will explain and develop the complexities in the ensuing chapters.

examples of actual student efforts, and some exercises to help you understand the concepts and develop the skills that you need to write each part of the paper effectively. At the end of each chapter, I will provide a practical summary to guide you through writing that section and remind you of the tentative calendar that guides you as you make slow and steady progress. Please remember, the research paper writing process takes time: time to develop a question, time to find appropriate sources, time to read and understand them, time to write, time to think, time to plan your research, time to conduct it, time to reflect on its significance, and finally, time to revise and edit it. Thus, work steadily on your project, following the deadlines that your professor provides for finishing each section.

When I teach my course, I ask the students to write their paper in four different installments. In the first, they hand in their Literature Review and Model and Hypothesis sections; for the second, revisions of their first paper are included along with a title and the Introduction and Research Design sections. In the third installment, they hand in a draft of the Analysis and Assessment section, again reworking the preceding parts of the paper, and for the last one, they write the Conclusion and present a revised final paper. As an additional guide for my students, I provide them with a Writing Checklist that they fill out before handing in each installment. I have included these for your use at the end of the appropriate chapter. As you will see, these checklists follow directly from the Practical Summaries. You should think of them as rubrics for your own papers and should consult them as you work through your sections.

The design of my course and this book might be striking to some because I require my students to begin writing as soon as possible. This recommendation may seem counterintuitive. "How can I write when I am still learning about a subject?" most students ask. The response is that writing is part of the thinking process, and you cannot make adequate intellectual advances without starting to write, and therefore, think, from the outset. By the end of the process, you will have a draft that looks very different from the first one that you wrote, but that final version that you put forth is a product of the thinking and learning that you did all project long. If you do not put your initial thoughts on paper, then you are not likely to remember them and will not produce the same work as you would have had you begun writing earlier. This book encourages (and, in fact, demands) that you write your research paper in pieces, beginning with the first substantive parts of the paper and revising continually as you proceed. Insisting on writing from the outset makes clear a distinction that most students also don't recognize: **revising** and **editing** are different processes. Revising entails rethinking and major rewriting, whereas editing consists of fixing grammatical errors, format mistakes, and varying word choice.

BLUEPRINT OF THE BOOK

In the paragraphs that follow, I will briefly explain the contents of each chapter of the book. I recommend that you read this now to gain a better general understanding of the research paper writing process. If you like, come back to these discussions prior to reading each chapter as a way to help you focus on the main tasks to be accomplished in that section.

In Chapter 2, we take up the challenge of determining a "good" research question. Posing a question that is interesting and important to you, scholars, policy makers, and the average citizen is the key to a "good" choice. As you will see, coming up with an interesting query is perhaps the hardest and most important part of the project. It sets the stage for the whole research paper. As we consider what makes a compelling question, we will note the diversity of kinds of research in which one may be engaged as a political scientist. And you will meet five students whose interests and research topics will reappear at different points in the book. You will even see excerpts of some of these students' efforts to give you examples of how others *like you* have handled the distinct tasks involved in writing a research paper.

After identifying a research question, you are ready to look at how others, namely scholars, have answered similar queries.[7] In Chapter 3, you begin work on the second phase of your project: determining and understanding the academic debate. In this section, you need to discover how scholars answer your *general* research question. The emphasis here is on identifying the different **schools of thought** or answers to the question and making sure that you have included the most important scholarly voices on the subject. A school of thought is united by a common approach, such as pointing to a particular factor as the key cause or sharing a methodology.

You conclude your literature review with a **thesis,** the answer to your research question. For empirical research, this thesis has to be

---

[7]Some undergraduate papers in Political Theory may not include a literature review of secondary sources. Look to your instructor for guidance on how she or he wants you to handle the task of identifying and classifying different perspectives.

developed further to guide you through the rest of your project. Chapter 4 then helps you translate this thesis into a **model** and **hypothesis.** A model is a kind of flow diagram that identifies the cause(s) and effect as concepts and asserts graphically that X → Y (where X leads to Y). While the model helps you focus on the key factors that you will need to study, it does not specify exactly how they are related. Does Y increase if X decreases? Because you cannot tell from the model, you need the hypothesis. The hypothesis identifies the ways in which these factors are related, and is typically stated as "the more of X, the less of Y," if you are positing a *negative relationship* between two *continuous variables.* (If you were expecting a *positive relationship,* the sentence would read, "the more of X, the more of Y.")[8]

Once you have surveyed the scholarly literature and developed a model and hypothesis, you take a step back, in effect, to write an Introduction and a working title. Chapter 5 guides you through these efforts. You will use what you have accomplished in identifying a question to entice people to read your paper. In addition to defining and justifying your research question, the introduction provides the writer and reader a "road map" or "snapshot" of the whole paper. Thus, the Introduction requires that you map out the different parts of the project and make some educated guesses about what you will find. (Note that in the final draft of this section, you no longer include "guesses," but report the actual findings.) Because you have completed the Literature Review and Model and Hypothesis sections, you will be able to state clearly the scholarly debate and the answer that you think is most compelling. Trying to map out the rest of the paper at this point is difficult, but not impossible. You have a general understanding of the other sections (Research Design, Analysis and Assessment, and Conclusion), and the sooner you start conceiving of each of the pieces and their relationships to the whole, the easier it will be to perform the research and write the final product. The title should

---

[8]The alternative is if the variables are noncontinuous or discrete (also referred to as category variables, which can come in unranked versions called **nominal**—like sex or religion—or ranked versions called **ordinal**—such as educational achievement of primary, secondary, some college, college graduate, or postgraduate). With discrete variables, the basic hypothesis would read something like the following: "If X is A, then Y is B, but if X is C, then Y is D." For instance, following from the work of Juan J. Linz and Arturo Valenzuela on the relationship between types of governmental systems and the consolidation of democracy, a hypothesis would read: "If the governmental system is presidential, then consolidation is less likely, but if the governmental system is a parliamentary one, then consolidation is more likely." See Linz and Valenzuela, *The Limits of Presidential Democracy* (Baltimore: Johns Hopkins University Press, 1994). Please note that we will discuss types of data—nominal, ordinal, and interval—in more detail in Chapter 6.

accomplish goals similar to the Introduction, but in miniature. A good title will communicate in an interesting way the puzzle (which may include the actual cases in which you are interested) as well as your answer, in a few phrases, so the reader will know what you are writing about and what you are arguing.

After completing a draft of your Introduction and coming up with a compelling title, you will tackle the third task delineated in Table 1.1: evaluating the appropriateness of the answers that you identified in the Literature Review. This evaluation maps into two different parts of the research paper. Chapter 6 walks you through the first one, the Research Design. In this section, you design your "evaluation" or "test" of your thesis, and this undertaking is multifaceted. Here you explicitly state how you will translate the concepts into identifiable or measurable entities. In addition, you determine what set of cases you need to study in order to assess the thesis or model and hypothesis. Carefully considering sources and data is important here, and you will see how the kind of information that you need at this stage is very different from what you relied on earlier. Finally, you explain exactly how you will generate your information, for example identifying how you will know what "values" your variables take on or providing a sample survey if you plan to administer one.

Throughout this section, you acknowledge any weaknesses and profess any compromises you had to make in designing your project because of the difficulty in finding adequate measures for a concept or obtaining the best data. In a sense, in this section, you write your own contract and insurance policy for the project. You tell the readers: this is what I'm going to achieve and why. I may not be able to get access to the precise information that I would need to evaluate this question, but this is the best I have.

In his classic textbook in methodology, W. Phillips Shively notes with tongue in cheek that Political Science is not rocket science. Natural scientists and engineers have verifiable physical laws that have been shown to hold and describe the situations in which they are interested, as well as instruments that can precisely measure the phenomena they are investigating. In Political Science, we have few laws, difficulty translating key concepts into measurable entities, and trouble collecting or getting access to "good" data. Thus, as Shively notes, Political Science is not rocket science—it's *much* harder![9]

---

[9] W. Phillips Shively, *The Craft of Political Research*, 5th ed. (Upper Saddle Brook, NJ: Prentice Hall, 2002), p. 17.

In Chapter 7, you continue with the task of evaluation. Now that you have planned your project carefully and explained why you made the choices that you did, you are finally ready to examine the facts or logic related to the case. This is the part of the paper about which students are most excited; this is also what most students conceive of (prior to learning what a research paper really is) as the only important part of the paper. However, as I hope to show throughout this book, the Analysis and Assessment section[10] of the paper cannot stand alone. It only makes sense and carries weight after you have performed the other tasks. Moreover, by surveying the literature, developing a thesis or model and hypothesis, and carefully designing the research, you are in a better position to write a focused and convincing assessment of the evidence, principles, and/or logic that can sway a reader to hold the same view that you do.

Chapter 8 provides you with a guide to writing a good conclusion, the fourth task to be accomplished. Just like the marathoner, you cannot simply give up at Mile 22, limp to the finish line, and feel satisfied. You need to complete the race/paper strongly. You've run/written more than most people have, but you aren't done yet. You need an effective conclusion that ties the whole project together, considers the implications of your findings, and poses questions for future research. If your research has gone forward with few complications—you have been able to find the data that you wanted and you have clear evidence to support your contentions—then the

---

[10]Throughout the book, I will try to address some of the controversies and rivalries that divide quantitative and qualitative researchers. Some contend that typical social science terminology privileges and encourages quantitative types of analysis over qualitative ones. I will attempt to be agnostic in this debate, while trying to avoid favoring any approach. Although I think that it is important for undergraduates to be exposed to both kinds of analysis, I assert that the vast majority of undergraduate political scientists are majors because they are excited about the kinds of things that they can learn through *qualitative analysis*. Moreover, the vast majority of Political Science undergraduate faculty do not themselves engage in quantitative research. Thus, why assume that research paper writing and a discussion of methodology at the undergraduate level must be quantitative? In fact, this book project is driven by the notion that methodology should not be divorced from the rest of the curriculum. Research methods and research paper writing should be seen as integral parts of a Political Science major, a bridge between the introductory courses that identify questions and schools of thought and more advanced classes and seminars that ask students to focus on a particular area of study and think like a scholar themselves. For others who have advocated such a view see John C. Wahlke, "Liberal Learning and the Political Science Major: A Report to the Profession," *PS: Political Science and Politics* 24 (March 1991): 48–60. An empirical study of learning outcomes that notes the utility of such an approach is John Ishiyama, "Examining the Impact of the Wahlke Report: Surveying the Structure of the Political Science Curricula at Liberal Arts and Sciences Colleges and Universities in the Midwest," *PS: Political Science and Politics* 38 (January 2005): 71–74.

conclusion reminds the reader of what you have achieved, explains why these accomplishments are important, and considers both the limits of the research and whether this project provides insights that are applicable to other situations. The conclusion is also where you have a chance to set out questions that you would like to answer if you continue this research. But if your project has been frustrating— i.e. you do not have conclusive findings to report or the evidence requires that you reject your hypothesis—you need to consider why you have the findings you do and whether anything can be done to salvage your initial argument. Regardless of whether your hypothesis was confirmed, rejected, or the jury is still out, your conclusion identifies future paths for continued research.

Finally, you need to spend time revising and editing the paper. This is your last mile. The paper is almost done, but it is not complete, because a final draft is a polished one. You can only turn in a polished paper if you carefully check to make sure that each section accomplishes what it should, that the paper is well written, and that you have followed all of the formatting instructions that your professor has specified.

So, now that we have specified the tasks to be completed and the parts of the research paper that have to be written, we have begun the process of demystifying the Political Science research paper. Whenever you find yourself getting foggy on the process and the goals, turn back to Table 1.1 and remind yourself:

> To write this research paper, I have to accomplish *five tasks* and I have to write *six distinct sections.* Each of these sections has a definite purpose and a set of tasks that I can accomplish. And after I finish each one, I can check them off as a "completed draft." Moreover, in the Practical Summaries and the Writing Checklists at the end of the chapters, I have precise recommendations regarding what I have to do to finish each section. Thus, every part of the paper becomes manageable, particularly if I work on this project over a period of time. In fact, I have a suggested calendar for completing each of the five tasks. Thus, if I follow the directions and the advice spelled out here, I can turn in a paper that is compelling to any reader and of which I will be proud. In effect, then, if I am the Tortoise and proceed slowly and steadily, I will win the race!

2

Getting Started: Finding a Research Question

S tarting a research project is truly a formidable task. It is challenging because good research topics are usually very specific and, in fact, not topics at all, but rather questions or puzzles. In this chapter, I will define the characteristics of a good research question and walk you through a variety of ways of finding one.

CHARACTERISTICS OF ''GOOD'' QUESTIONS

All great research questions share four qualities, and you can use these criteria to help you generate a topic and then transform it into a question for study.[1] Research questions are *interesting, important,* and *puzzling* to at least three and hopefully four different audiences—to you, scholars, the public policy community, and, ideally, ordinary citizens. Lastly, a good question is *short and direct*: If you need multiple lines or sentences to state your query then you still have some work to do refining it into one that captures people's attention and concisely identifies a puzzle.

---

[1]There is actually a fifth criterion, that the research is "do-able." By "do-able" I mean that the student can actually answer this question and finish this paper with the resources available. We will discuss this characteristic in more detail in the Research Methods section, as we explore, especially, operationalization and case selection. See Chapter 6.

Find Something Interesting

OK, great, I've given you criteria, but now how do you satisfy them? First, how do you find something that is interesting *to you*? Some students are really excited about a topic, and for them, picking a general area of research is easy. For others, this task is more of a challenge, but here are some strategies to help. One method is to write down what motivated you to become a Political Science major. Let's use the experiences of some students to illustrate this approach. Imagine that there is a student named Latisha who wants to run for office. She decided to major in Political Science and go to law school because she thought that sequence was the best path for achieving her goals. Another student, Matt, got involved in Political Science because he was fascinated by recent presidential elections. Then there is Diana, who came to the field because of the 2003 Iraq War. She is interested in the problem of the proliferation of weapons of mass destruction (WMD), how best to slow the spread of such technology, and the U.S.-led war with Iraq. The lists of topics for our three hypothetical students look like this:

Latisha	Matt	Diana
Electoral politics	2000 & 2004	2003 Iraq War
Law	Presidential	Proliferation of WMD
	Elections	Anti-proliferation policy

Other students may have arrived at the major in a very different manner. They may have been attracted by a great course or professor. What courses have you enjoyed in the discipline? Or, even better, what segments of your favorite courses did you like the best? Imagine that Tom really liked his course in urban politics, particularly the segment on the politics of economic development. He's a baseball fan, and he's very interested in the impact of new sports stadiums on the economies of their host cities. Tom can then make the following list:

Tom
Urban politics
Economic development
Sports stadiums and their economic impact

Students often choose Political Science as a major because they are fascinated with current events and the news. Kate is one such student who likes to read news stories about women and gender. She can begin her list, too.

Kate

Women

Gender

If you don't have an issue in mind that you would like to research, you can use the approaches that Latisha, Matt, Diana, Tom, or Kate chose. Just use the following questions to help you develop a topic:

1. What piqued your interest in politics?
2. Why did you become a Political Science major?
3. In what current events or news stories are you most interested?

Then, regardless of how you arrived at your topic, you should try to justify *why* you think the subjects on your list are interesting. As you think of why these issues are appealing, try to write down some questions that you have about your topics. If the hypothetical students follow my advice, they will create lists that look something like those reported in Table 2.1.

Hopefully, you can see that a little brainstorming can move you forward considerably on the path to finding a research question that is interesting to you.

Determining Why Your Topic Is Important

Along with being interesting, your research question should be *important* to you and a larger community of scholars, policy makers and citizens. You may doubt that your particular interest—baseball stadiums as growth engines for cities—could be important, but you will be pleasantly surprised to learn that many people share your curiosity. To identify the level of scholarly interest, you can look up your topic in an *online database* of academic articles. Some excellent databases for this purpose include *Academic Search Premier* (from Ebscohost Research Databases), *Journal Storage: The Scholarly Archive*, more popularly known as JSTOR, and *ProQuest Research Library*. These can help you locate articles in the premier journals in Political Science,

TABLE 2.1 Transforming a Topic into a Research Question: How Five Students Progressed?

	Latisha	Matt	Diana	Tom	Kate
Topics	Electoral politics Law	2000 & 2004 elections	2003 Iraq War WMD proliferation Anti-proliferation policy	Urban politics Downtown development Sports stadiums and their economic impact	Women Gender
Why interesting?	I want to run for office/go to law school	I am puzzled with/angered by the controversy over the 2000 outcome. I am also interested in the enormous increase in voter turnout in 2004.	WMD proliferation frightens me. I'd like to find ways to slow proliferation. I wonder how the Iraq war works as an anti-proliferation strategy.	I like sports and enjoy the new stadiums. I would like to think that these produce a larger good for the city. I like cities and want to think about ways of revitalizing them and keeping them vibrant.	I never understood why gender inequality persists; I am frustrated that so much of the news is about (male) elites. I want to learn more about ordinary people who might not be very empowered.
Related questions	How do candidates get elected? What roles do lawyers play in the political process?	Why was the Supreme Court able to decide the case as it did? Why did anyone seek to question the 2000 FL vote? Should the Electoral College be so important? Why did so many voters participate in 2004? Why wasn't the outcome as close in 2004 as in 2000?	Why do states or groups seek WMD? What policies work to slow WMD proliferation? What effect has the Iraq War had on proliferation? Was the Iraq War about proliferation?	What policies work to keep cities vibrant? Why are some cities successful and others not? Are there "smart" or good development formulas? How can sports or entertainment help foster positive economic growth for all urban residents?	Where is there still gender inequality today? Why does gender inequality exist? Why aren't females more empowered?

17

as well as related fields such as Economics, History, Sociology, and various area studies. You may want to start by reading several book reviews or article abstracts to get a better sense of why academics find this subject important.

Students are too willing these days to rely exclusively on sources they can read on or print from their computer. While online materials are wonderful, there's a wealth of knowledge that you can acquire in the library. First of all, books are extremely important repositories of knowledge, and you typically cannot get access to full-length scholarly works online. In addition, older and sometimes more recent issues of some journals might not be available electronically. Moreover, databases index different subsets of journals. You may have chosen a database to search that doesn't include one of the most important journals for your topic. So, be sure to use your library's online catalog to find books and the major journals concerned with your topic, go to the library, and actually poke around. If you find a good book or journal, chances are that shelved near that source you will find several other interesting and useful ones, too. And of course, you should let the first sources that you identify lead you to other ones. Look at what these authors cite as key works and be sure to read these books and articles, too.

For some help determining whether and why your topic is significant to ordinary people, you can brainstorm and come up with reasons on your own. You can also consult news articles and opinion pieces on these subjects. Journalists write with the general reader in mind and explain the importance of the news to members of the community. Editorial writers and columnists also make the case for the larger significance of events or policies. How do you find these types of articles? Here you can search using **Lexis-Nexis** as well as Academic Search Premier or ProQuest. Notice that in any of these databases, you can often specify the magazine, journal of opinion, newspaper or type of paper, and type of article (news, editorial, op-ed) along with the subject you are searching. When using these news sources be aware of both the audience for whom the authors are writing and any ideological leanings. For instance, you will find different political perspectives in *The Weekly Standard*, *The New Republic*, *The American Prospect*, and *The Economist*. You will also find varied coverage from newspapers that see themselves as national—i.e. the *New York Times*, *Washington Post*, or *Wall Street Journal*—versus local—the *Philadelphia Inquirer* or the *Rocky Mountain News*. All kinds of sources are valid for discovering the significance of your topic, but you need to be mindful of the intended audience and ideological leanings of the publication.

After you have done some research on why your issue is important, add to your list what you have discovered. If you are taking an idea from another writer, be sure that you note who the source of that point was.[2] Later, if you use this idea in your paper, you will want to be able to provide a full citation to that article.

Identifying a Puzzle and Using It to Frame a Question

So, you have found a topic that is interesting to you and that you know is important to others. Like our hypothetical students, your issue at this point may be too broad to proceed. The notion that you need to *narrow* a topic might seem strange. Typically, students are worried about finding enough information for their papers, so they think they need an expansive subject for which they can gather lots of facts. Here again, students are being misled by the misconception that the paper is purely a descriptive piece. Your paper is not a story about the "who, what, where, and when" of politics, your paper is an analytic effort that (usually) answers *"why, how, to what extent,* or *under what conditions."* Another way to think of your goal is that your paper seeks to resolve some puzzle in Political Science. What could be puzzling about politics, or what is a puzzle in Political Science? Well, I'm not talking about a jigsaw puzzle or Rubik's cube, but rather an event or development that doesn't seem to make sense; in other words, a phenomenon that is surprising given what we know about politics. Another way of thinking about this kind of intellectual dilemma is that it either lacks obvious answers or the conventional wisdom appears to be incorrect.

In framing their questions, students often want to pose and then answer one that begins with "should," "ought," or "what should." Questions that start this way—"normative queries"—are excellent ones for the sub-field of Political Theory. Typically, such papers try to determine what the best approach is given a set of principles defined by great political thinkers. If you are writing your paper for a Political Theory class, then answering a should, ought, or what should question is precisely what you should be doing. However, if you are writing your paper for a course in a different **sub-field** or for a research methods class, then you are usually supposed to be engaged in empirical Political Science. In other words, your job is to use **data** (i.e., observable facts or information) to evaluate

---

[2]I'll discuss the importance of giving credit to sources and avoiding plagiarism in more detail in Chapter 3.

some theory or hypothesis or to assess some public policy solution. For this, you must reframe your normative question into an empirical one. Luckily, reformulating isn't hard. For instance, Kate could be puzzling about what the nations of the world should do to promote gender equality. One way to transform this into an empirical question is to make it a policy-oriented one, focused on one or more solutions to the lack of female empowerment. Kate has found that in some of the least developed countries, international institutions have put into place a practice of microlending (the making of very small loans to ordinary people that allow them to establish their own businesses) as a way of both promoting development and reducing gender inequalities. She could ask: Under what conditions do these microlending policies work to enhance women's political power? Or, if she leans toward theory-oriented research, Kate might wonder: Why does the political power of women vary around the world? Thus, the normative question can easily inspire two other types of question, the public policy "under what conditions" and the theory-oriented "why" query.

Throughout this text, I will be encouraging students to engage in three different kinds of research: **theory-oriented**, **public policy**, and **political theory**.[3] Theory-oriented and public-policy research are both **empirical**. Empirical means that researchers use information or data (facts, figures) as evidence to answer their research question. In contrast, Political Theory is nonempirical or **normative**, as it investigates what should or ought to be or the meanings and implications of the works of great political thinkers.

Americanists, Comparativists, and students of International Politics typically are engaged in either public policy or theory-oriented research. What distinguishes one from the other is the extent to which the research helps solve a particular problem. Public-policy research is applied, meaning that it will investigate how to solve problems, such as how to design a well-functioning political system in a certain cultural setting, or how to create a well-performing city school system in the United States. Theory-oriented research, in contrast, explores why politics is the way it is, without reference to any

---

[3]These terms come (with slight adjustments in nomenclature) from W. Phillips Shively. He identifies four kinds of research—normative philosophy (political theory), formal theory, engineering (public policy), and theory-oriented—divided along two dimensions: nonempirical versus empirical and applied versus basic. For most undergraduates, formal theory papers are beyond their interest and the scope of their training, so I will not deal with them explicitly here. Shively, *The Craft of Political Research*, 5th ed. (Upper Saddle River, NJ: Prentice Hall, 2002), pp. 4–6.

particular problem to be solved. While there may be practical applications for theory-oriented research, the ultimate policy spin-offs are not what motivate these inquiries.[4]

So, as you work to transform your topic and your questions into researchable ones, remember that your preferred type of query will vary depending on the course for which you are writing this paper or the purpose of the research. For most empirical courses, you will be encouraged to conduct theory-oriented or public-policy research, and for theory courses, you will engage in normative work. With these requirements in mind, then, let's return to the topics and ideas generated by our hypothetical students and try to think of puzzles for them to solve. The future attorney and politician, Latisha, might want to investigate whether lawyers make good law makers or understand why some candidates win elections while others lose. Matt, who was drawn to Political Science by recent elections, might ask the following: Why did voter turnout increase substantially in 2004? To what extent have the Republicans consolidated their power at all levels of American government? Still mulling over the 2000 election and puzzling over the fact that the top voter-getter in the election was the loser, Matt might want to ask whether the Electoral College should continue to be the arbiter of presidential contests.

Another set of puzzles follows from Diana's interests: Why do states and other groups seek weapons of mass destruction? What policies have worked in the past to slow WMD proliferation? Was the Iraq War about slowing proliferation or something else? What effect has the Iraq War had on anti-proliferation efforts around the globe? Turning to Tom, he could decide to explore the conditions under which big urban projects—such as sports stadiums, entertainment zones, or convention centers—have a positive impact on the local economy. Lastly, Kate might ask what accounts for the varying success rates of women in electoral politics in different countries of the world or at different levels of government in the United States.

Most of the questions that I generated here would lead to theory-oriented research. If you were interested in a policy question, a good way to develop one is to evaluate existing solutions that have been enacted to address some public challenge. If Latisha is looking for a public policy question in the area of voting behavior, she might want to look at "Motor Voter Laws," which gave citizens the ability to register to vote when they got or renewed their drivers' licenses.

---

[4]Ibid.

The idea behind this law was that the difficulty in signing up for the voter rolls was preventing many people from participating in elections. So, officials mused, making voter registration easier would allow more people to vote. Latisha could then generate a public policy question examining the extent to which Motor Voter "worked." Have more people registered? Are more people voting? Why or why not? In public policy research, solutions to problems create opportunities for more research, as analysts seek to evaluate the policy results and offer new and better answers to these challenges.

Through brainstorming and a little bit of early research, our students have good starts on finding some kind of puzzle that they might be interested in solving, as Table 2.2 (which is a continuation of their lists) shows.

What the students need to do now is to identify or develop questions with the help of their lists, considering the requirements of their courses. For papers in the sub-fields of American, Comparative, or International Politics, the questions should generally start with "Why," "How," "To what extent," or "Under what conditions." For Political Theory papers, students should ask "Should," "Ought," "What should," "What ought," or "What did the concept 'x' mean for theorist 'Y'."

Stating Your Question Concisely and Directly

When you can state a research question in one of these appropriate forms, then you, too, are on your way to a good paper. But you're not done yet. Have you ever gone to a public lecture and noticed that many questioners take too long in posing their query to the speaker? Are you often frustrated listening to that audience member go on about his issue before stating the question? If you answered yes to these two questions, then you have an instinctual understanding of the fourth characteristic of a good research question: It is short and direct. You want to identify a puzzle and ask about it as briefly and straightforwardly as possible. For instance, notice the differing impact of two questions that Kate could ask:

Example Question A

The idea of and movement for female political equality and the women's movement was born in the United States in the 19th century. The United States is also the birthplace of modern democracy, and a society in which liberal values are pervasive. Still, U.S. women have not done that well in elections,

T A B L E 2.2 Transforming a Topic into a Research Question, Part II

	Latisha	Matt	Diana	Tom	Kate
Why important?	Elections determine our leaders; why do some candidates win and others lose? Many elected officials are lawyers. To what extent does legal training make them better law makers?	Voting is an important act in democracy; many were bemoaning nonparticipation. Does the 2004 turnout suggest a healthier U.S. democracy? Gore won the popular vote yet lost the election in 2000. Because of the Electoral College, candidates focus enormous attention on the few states that are "up for grabs." Is this the best way for deciding who will be the U.S. President?	As of late 2005, about 2000 Americans and far more Iraqis have died in the war. No clear evidence of WMD has been found, and Iran, North Korea, and al Qaeda are all still trying to develop WMD.	Cities are still important centers of commerce and culture, if not of manufacturing. What happens in urban centers affects not only cities, but bordering regions. Cities tend to be places where the very privileged and the very underprivileged mingle. We should have some commitment to the poorest in our society.	Women make up more than half the world's population, yet they tend to be poorer and more powerless than men. Women also tend to be responsible for children; when women's conditions are poor, then so too are children's. Is there hypocrisy when some contend that all people have equal rights today?

compared to women in other parts of the world, particularly in certain European states, but also in some Asian countries. I don't think that American democracy is working that well.

Example Question B

Why are the rates of electoral success of American women lower than those of females in some other countries?

In the first example, Kate spends too much time explaining the puzzle and making a political statement. In fact, she never actually asks a question. Question B is preferable because it so nicely and concisely states the query. Seek that brief and direct question and recognize that you will have plenty of time in your Introduction to explain why your query is interesting, important, and puzzling.

STILL STUCK? WHAT TO DO IF DESPITE THESE IDEAS, YOU NONETHELESS LACK A QUESTION

Perhaps my ideas for generating a topic and a question have not helped you yet. You don't really know why you're a Political Science major, or my suggestions for generating a topic from your courses or from the headlines haven't helped you come up with anything particularly inspiring. If this is the case for you, then I would suggest that you pick one of your introductory courses—whichever was your favorite, or if you had no favorite, simply pick one. Find your books and notes for that course. If you tend to sell your books back at the end of the semester, I strongly advise you NOT to exchange the ones from your major, especially the introductory texts. You get relatively little money back, and these are excellent resources for the rest of your academic career. Hold on to your notes as well. Your faculty members use their time to provide you with the information they believe is essential for mastering a subject. Do not just throw this wisdom away at the end of the term. Remember, you are supposed to be *cumulating knowledge and skills* throughout your college career—building on what you have learned before—and your books and notes are the foundations from which you build. If you were a foreign language major, you could not survive a literature class without first achieving language proficiency. So, too, should you think about your own field of study as a cumulative endeavor. Your Political Science courses are building on each other; you are not simply learning a set of facts about different countries, institutions, time periods, public policies, political philosophies, or interstate interactions. So, keep your books to consult as you take advanced courses in the major. If you have no textbooks now, however, go to your library and check one out (or, as a last resort, go to your professor and see if you can borrow one). Textbooks and readers are extremely useful sources not only for question generation but for the next stage of the research process, the phase of determining how different scholars have studied your puzzle.

If your favorite introductory class was American Government and Politics, then you should open up your American Government textbook. I am looking at two very popular and widely used ones— Welch, Gruhl, Comer, and Rigdon, *American Government*, 9th ed. (Belmont, CA: Wadsworth/Thomson Learning, 2004) and Sidlow and Henschen, *America at Odds*, 4th ed. (Belmont, CA: Wadsworth/ Thomson Learning, 2004). (If neither of these was your textbook, *you can still use your former text in a way similar to what I am going to describe*.) First, open the textbook to the short version of the Table of Contents (in Welch et al. it's called "Brief Contents" and in Sidlow and Henschen it's "Contents in Brief"). This provides an outline of the book in a nutshell. And that quick look shows you that the books cover similar topics. There's a first part on the basics of the American system, with a discussion of its historical development, and then the rest of the book examines the actors (interest groups, parties, media, etc.) and the institutions (congress, presidency, bureaucracy, and judiciary). Both books also have special sections on civil liberties and rights and public policy (with some variation on the type of policy covered).

Perhaps just looking at these topics will help you remember what parts of your book and course you found interesting. Suppose that, for you, it was the "Civil Rights and Liberties" section of the book. If you open up to the first pages of these chapters, you are met with controversial and timely issues. For Welch et al., there's a photograph of a boy scout, who has publicly stated that he is gay, and opposite it is the question "Can the Boy Scouts Discriminate Against Homosexuals?" (pp. 420, 421). In Sidlow and Henschen, there is one picture of a protest event showing a person holding a sign that says "Big Brother is Watching" and another looking at the Bill of Rights with a magnifying glass (p. 73). Under this picture, the authors tell you that in this chapter you will learn (among other things) why Americans are increasingly concerned about privacy rights. The next page (p. 74) asks "Should Hate Speech on Campus be Banned?" Both these texts, then, provide you with pictures and questions that can help you to produce some interesting ideas of your own for a research paper. Perhaps you're now inspired to examine cases of *legal* discrimination. Or you might want to make an argument about why court rulings around these issues have evolved as they have. Another possibility is to investigate some related, local developments, for instance the extent to which officials on *your campus* restrict speech. A last idea for empirical work is to examine the politics of the Patriot Act and Patriot II. Why was one passed so easily and the other met with more opposition?

The topic of civil rights and liberties can also lead to normative inquiries. You could ask, for instance, whether women's health clubs *should be* able to deny membership based on sex. Or you could examine whether campus officials *should be* allowed to restrict speech. Another possible question is to identify the conditions under which the federal government *should be* permitted to invade citizens' privacy in the fight against terrorism. Lastly, you could consider whether Patriot I and/or Patriot II *should be* the law of the land.

Hopefully, working through these examples shows you that your own old textbooks can spark your interest and spur you on to come up with different kinds of research questions. Of course, there might not be pictures or controversial headings in the chapters where you begin searching. If that is the case, read the text and see what the authors have to say about this topic and why it continues to be interesting and important. This discussion will likely address topics that might pique your curiosity and inspire questions. At the end of the chapters, the authors usually provide suggestions for further reading—other articles, books, and websites. You can consult these works for more help. You can also go back to your notes from this section of the course and see what your professor had to say about this topic. If you had additional readings, those are great, too, because often those materials are, in effect, research papers that scholars or policy makers have written on related subjects.

In sum, the chapters in your textbooks help you understand why these topics are interesting, important, and puzzling to our desired audiences—you, scholars, practitioners, and ordinary citizens. Thus, they can be great sources of inspiration for research questions. You must remember, however, that nowhere in the text will there be a flashing neon light that says "Here's a great question; take it!" Instead, you have to read and think to develop your query, regardless of which method you use. But the more actively you engage in this endeavor, the better suited to your interests will be the question that you develop. By working hard to arrive at a question, you will find an area of research that you find fascinating, and thus you will have a positive experience writing your paper.

PRACTICAL SUMMARY

In this chapter, you have learned about what makes a good research question and the different kinds of research in which political scientists typically engage. Excellent research questions are interesting, important, puzzling, and brief. For undergraduates, research projects can be empirical (theory oriented or public policy) or nonempirical (political theory), although there tends to be a bias in research methods classes toward theory-oriented or public-policy papers. The type of question that you ask is often not dependent on the topic but on the course or the purpose for which you are writing the paper. In other words, you can develop many different kinds of research questions from one topic.

The chapter also provided several methods for generating research questions. We met five students (who will return in other chapters of this book as we work through different stages of the research process) who are learning how to discover interesting topics and transform them into actual questions. Finding such a query often takes some effort, but it is not impossible, especially if you follow the advice outlined here. Perhaps the hardest part in determining the question is uncovering a source of inspiration. I have suggested four: (a) why you became interested in Political Science; (b) a favorite course or a favorite part of a class that you have had; (c) current events; and (d) textbooks.[5] Once you have a source, I suggest that you do the following things:

1. Identify a *topic* that is interesting to you

2. Write down *why* that topic is interesting to you and think of why it might be interesting to others, too. (If you need help, you can consult outside sources here.)

3. Generate some *basic questions* related to your topic. These can be in any form.

---

[5]Of course, there are others. For instance, extracurricular activities and career aspirations are other sources of topics and, ultimately, questions. Moreover, once you have done some research of your own, you will have another source: your previous research. Typically, an analyst generates more questions every time she becomes involved in a project.

4. Write down why this topic is important to you and others. (Again, if you need help, you can consult outside sources here.)

5. Try to think about genuine puzzles involving this topic and then develop a related research question, that is, one that starts with *why, how, to what extent, should, or what should?*

6. Be sure that your question is *short,* one relatively simple sentence. If you need a paragraph or several lines of text to state your question, then you need to revise it, boiling it down to its puzzle.

7. Identify the type of research question you have posed. Be sure it is appropriate to the requirements of your class. If it is not, make adjustments.

8. Get approval of your research question from your instructor. If she suggests changes, modify the query and run the new question by her.

SUGGESTED CALENDAR

In the first week or two of classes, your professor will likely want you to perform the steps outlined in the Practical Summary section to identify one or more possible research questions. And, yes, you frequently need to start defining your question *that early.* I suggest that you generate more than one question because sometimes you may not be exactly sure what you want to study, and thinking of a few questions can help you clarify your ideas as well as give your instructor more to respond to as you refine your query. Clear your question with your professor and take any advice that she might give about revising it. Once your question is set, you are on your way!

EXERCISES

1. Develop a research question for each of our five students—Latisha, Matt, Diana, Tom, and Kate. As you create your list of five total questions, make sure that you have at least one theory-oriented, one public policy, and one political theory question. Be sure to identify which question is which.

2. Think of why you became a Political Science major or consider one of your favorite courses. Develop one theory-oriented, one

public-policy, and one political theory question based on your own experiences. Be sure to follow the proposed steps for each of the three queries:

    Topic:
    Why Interesting:
    Why Important:
    Related Questions:
    Research Question:

What kind of research question have you posed?

3. Pick up a recent newspaper. Develop a research question based on a news article. Be sure to follow the proposed steps:

    Topic:
    Why Interesting:
    Why Important:
    Related Questions:

What kind of research question have you posed?

4. Consult one of your introductory textbooks. Develop a research question with its help. Be sure to follow the proposed steps:

    Topic:
    Why Interesting:
    Why Important:
    Related Questions:

What kind of research question have you posed?

CHECKLIST FOR THE RESEARCH QUESTION

Below you will see a checklist to consult as you are developing your question. When you think you have a good query, see if you can check off each of the items. If you can't, you know that you have more work to do to formulate a good research question.

1. My question is *interesting* to me, scholars, policy makers, and citizens.   _____

2. My question is *important* to me, scholars, policy makers, and citizens.   _____

3. My question is *puzzling* to me, scholars, policy makers, and citizens.   _____

4. I have written in paragraph form why my question is interesting, important, and puzzling to me, scholars, policy makers, and citizens.   _____

5. My research question starts with why, how, to what extent, or under what conditions (for an empirical paper) or ought, should, what ought, what should, or what did a certain theorist mean by "x" (for a normative paper).   _____

6. My question is short and direct.   _____

3

Addressing the Scholarly Debate: The Literature Review

The literature review is an analysis of the ***scholarly debate*** on your research question in its most general, concise form.[1] Imagine if Matt, our student who became a Political Science major because he found the elections of 2000 and 2004 so compelling, decided that he wanted to explore why voter turnout in the United States declined steadily for several decades and then surged in 2004. His general question is then: How do we explain voter turnout in the United States? The literature review uncovers the *multiple answers* that scholars studying the same issue have given and groups these answers into **schools of thought**. In this section, the writer gives each school a **label**. These labels can be standards in the field or specific, new ones that the researcher develops.

Literature reviews are neither paragraph summaries of the works of different authors, nor descriptions of perspectives (i.e. basic approaches) in broad terms. They coherently lay out the different specific *answers* to

---

[1]Some political theory papers lack a literature review of secondary sources. Please ask your professor for guidance on how to handle the literature review if you are writing your research paper for a class in political thought.

the general question as well as analyze the logical strengths and weaknesses of these responses and note any similarities between them. At the end of the literature review, you should conclude by determining which school of thought makes the most compelling argument. You must, of course, defend your position. At this point in your career, you're better off choosing from among those approaches that you have discussed, as opposed to deriving your own answer. Left to develop their own perspective, most students want to combine all or several of the explanations into one. For methodological reasons, this smorgasbord approach is not desirable. Remember, you are looking for the best explanation, not a perfect one. The goal in social science is to explain patterns, not to account for all the details of a particular case.[2]

ANSWERING THE GENERAL QUESTION

The first time you hear "literature review," you may be somewhat confused. You are used to thinking of literature as something that you read for pleasure or in an English or foreign language class, and that term means fiction to you. Academics, however, use the word "literature" to refer to a scholarly body of work. "Still," you may be thinking, "I'm interested in explaining something really recent, and scholars will not have published on my topic yet." In making that objection you are confusing the specifics of your case with the underlying question that you are asking. The literature review seeks to understand scholarly perspectives on the fundamental *conceptual*, not case-specific, puzzle you are exploring. Thus, while the Bush-Kerry election may be what you want to investigate, the general phenomena in which you are interested may be: Why do certain candidates get elected and others lose? What accounts for U.S. voter turnout rates? How important are "moral values" to voters? Or even, should the Electoral College decide presidential contests? Scholars have addressed these questions before, and you will be able to find a lively debate for each of them.

---

[2]Because of the goal to arrive at a better understanding of general political phenomena, we also tend to prefer parsimonious explanations or models, i.e., ones that cite as few causal factors as possible. W. Lawrence Neuman, *Social Research Methods: Qualitative and Quantitative Approaches*, 5th ed. (New York: Allyn and Bacon, 2003), p. 42.

Because the literature review is an exploration of scholarly answers to the general question, you will be looking for a particular type of source for this part of the paper. Primarily, you need to rely on the work of academics. While journalists and commentators may provide interesting answers and insights into your question, they should not be the authors that you cite at this stage. Your literature review must survey the *scholarly* literature. Who are scholars and where can you find their work? Scholars tend to be professors (working at universities or colleges) or people employed by think tanks and public policy and governmental institutes. These people usually publish their work in books (often, but not exclusively, ones that are published at university presses, textbook publishers, think tanks, and under certain imprints of large publishing houses) and in what are called peer-reviewed journals, periodicals with a policy of sending any piece that comes in for consideration out to other experts to review and approve. Academic journals publish a varying number of issues a year, but aren't weekly like *The Economist*, for instance. Scholarly journals tend to have footnotes and bibliographies. More policy-oriented journals (e.g. *Social Policy, Foreign Affairs,* or *Current History*) may lack the list of sources, but the articles that appear in them can be extremely relevant and are peer-reviewed.

You can find excellent books on your topic by searching your University's online catalogue. To locate the premier journals in Political Science, you can consult the online database JSTOR and select "browse" to view the Political Science journals. While these are not the only journals that can help, this is a good first place for you to look. You will see a list of periodicals that are some of the most prestigious in the field. Other databases, like Academic Search Premier and ProQuest, also index many excellent Political Science journals, and you can find scholarly articles by selecting "peer-review" journals when you search. But if you just start blindly searching, separating the most important scholarly statements from less important ones will be a hard task. In your literature review you want to consult the most important authors and find the most accepted answers.

To help you find the best sources for your literature review, follow these four suggestions:

1. Recognize that there are *generic answers* in political science to "why" or "how" questions, as well as to "should" or "ought" queries.

2. Use your books and notes from your courses (especially from your introductory classes) to identify the major schools and theorists.

3. Then (and only then) locate the books and articles you have identified with the help of your materials from your previous classes.

4. Finally search your library for additional books and articles related to your research question.

Notice what I have *not* suggested: *I have not recommended that you perform a Google (or other Internet) search.* Your goal is to find *scholarly sources* that answer your research question. While the web is a fabulous source of information and you could ultimately find many of the same materials that you will uncover using the methods I suggest, you need a certain degree of knowledge to use the Internet wisely for scholarly research. You cannot trust that every article posted on the web is important or accurate.

This is also not the time to search for facts or turn to encyclopedia-type sources. An encyclopedia is fine for primary and secondary school reports, but report-writing is behind you. You are now to engage in the scholarly debate and process.

GENERIC SCHOOLS OF THOUGHT

First, I want to let you in on a little secret that most professional political scientists know, but fail to tell their students. Regardless of the subfield that you study—American, Comparative, International, or Political Theory –there are basically four schools of thought that exist if we seek to divide our answers by the type of cause.[3] I call these schools **"Institutionalism," "Economism,"** the

---

[3]There are, of course, other ways to conceive of schools of thought, and several influential political scientists have written important works that delineate the field in different ways. Ronald H. Chilcote notes state and systems theories, culture theories, developmental theories, class theories, and political economy theories (all of which can be subsumed into my categories). See Ch. 1 "Comparative Inquiry" in *Theories of Comparative Politics: The Search for a Paradigm Reconsidered*, 2nd ed. (Boulder: Westview Press, 1994), pp. 3–17. Other scholars have used the level of analysis approach. Two prominents ones include Kenneth N. Waltz, *Man, the State, and War: A Theoretical Analysis* (New York: Columbia University Press, 1959) and J. David Singer, "The Level of Analysis Problem in International Relations," in *The International System: Theoretical Essays*, ed. J. David Singer, Klaus Knorr, and Sidney Verba (Princeton: Princeton University Press, 1961), pp. 77–92. Another approach is to distinguish by ontology, for instance **rationalist** versus **interpretivist**. For beginning students seeking to understand cause and effect, I find classifying by the type of independent variable to be more helpful. I am sure some faculty will disagree with my variable-centered approach. Of course, some analysts reject this focus on causation.

"Power Approach," and **"Culturalism"**.[4] One might argue that there are three different, generic schools for questions beginning with "should" or "ought:" "Yes," "No," and "Sometimes or Maybe." If you were to look at these varying answers to normative questions, however, you would often find that adherents reach different conclusions because they contend that either institutions, economics, power, or culture drives politics. (Sometimes what distinguishes the answers to normative or public-policy questions are the values and preferences of the authors. In those cases, you must determine these core principles as you try to understand the fundamental bases of their position.)

I call the first of the generic schools of thought "Institutionalism." Institutionalists—whether Americanists, Comparativists, IR specialists, or Political Theorists—agree that institutions "matter," i.e. that institutions are the most important explanatory factor in Political Science. What are institutions? Institutions can be the elements and rules within a political system—e.g., the electoral system (first-past-the-post vs. proportional representation); the governmental system (presidential vs. parliamentary); the legal system and constitution—or they can be international in scope, such as the Nuclear Non-Proliferation Treaty and the World Trade Organization (WTO). What is important about institutions, according to institutionalists, is that they provide incentives that encourage some behaviors and discourage others. For all (citizens, elites, groups, or states, depending on one's subfield) in the system, institutions define how to win rewards and receive punishments, and thus they affect the players' actions.

This perspective leads to explanations focusing on the rules and the mechanics of politics. For instance, institutionalists have contended that low voter turnout in the United States occurs because of the laws and procedures for registration. They have claimed that voter registration was too difficult and that making it easy to register would increase participation. As another example, students of gender and politics have often pointed to institutions as the explanation for the different percentage of women in national legislatures in Western Europe and the United States. The European use of proportional representation—where parties create lists that rank order the candidates and voters choose parties when they go

---

[4]I have developed these terms and they likely will not please some folks because they are highly generic. My goal, however, was to allow students to see the similarities *across the sub-fields* and to begin to see general approaches. I struggled with the terminology so as not to privilege the sub-field that I, personally, know best—international politics. I am sure, however, that my grounding in that area is obvious to experienced readers, and I beg the forbearance of Americanists, Comparativists, and Political Theorists.

to the polls—is far more conducive to electing females than are first-past-the-post contests in the United States.[5] In Scandinavia, voters choose a party list (and often 40% or more of the candidates listed are women), while in the United States individual women have to win their party's nomination and then secure victory in a head-to-head contest in the general election. Thus, the rules make it easier for women to be elected in Scandinavia. In international relations, institutionalists claim that institutions affect the behavior of states.[6] For instance, regime theorists, one type of IR institutionalists, argue that states respond to the incentives provided by international institutions in selecting their policies.[7] Moreover, in Political Theory, liberals, as they are more commonly called, also have a normative preference for institutions, contending, for instance, that the appropriate contracts, laws, or constitution can provide the frameworks to structure behavior so that humans interact peacefully and prosperously.

A second set of scholars would accept the by-now famous slogan of Bill Clinton's first presidential campaign: "It's the economy, stupid." Economic determinists[8] think that economic conditions drive politics. These scholars might argue that richer countries are more likely to be democratic than poorer ones or that American cities tend to be limited in their development options because of the financial constraints under which they operate.[9] In the realm of international politics, some economic determinists argue that the American wars with Iraq have been

---

[5]Pippa Norris and Ronald Inglehart, "Cultural Obstacles to Equal Representation," *Journal of Democracy* 12, no. 3 (2001): 130.

[6]Robert O. Keohane and Lisa L. Martin, "The Promise of Institutionalist Theory," *International Security* 20, no. 1 (1995): 39–51. In international relations, you are also likely to see this group of scholars referred to as "liberals," "liberal institutionalists," "neo-liberals" or "idealists." I have used this term "institutionalist" here, however, in order to be able to think of the whole field of political science. Conversely, in political theory, you would be more likely to see these people referred to as "liberals."

[7]Robert Keohane, *After Hegemony: Cooperation and Discord in the World Political Economy* (Princeton: Princeton University Press, 1984). Also most of the articles in Stephen D. Krasner, ed. *International Regimes* (Ithaca: Cornell University Press, 1983) make that argument.

[8]We can refer to this as the "Economist" school, but I prefer **not** calling its adherents "Economists," because Economists are generally known as professionals with advanced training in the academic discipline of Economics.

[9]Some examples of various works in this school include: Seymour Martin Lipset, *Political Man: The Social Bases of Politics* (Baltimore: Johns Hopkins University Press, 1981), Adam Przeworski and Fernando Limongi Neto, "Modernization: Theories and Facts," *World Politics* 49, no. 2 (1997): 155–183, Walt W. Rostow, *Stages of Economic Growth: A Non-Communist Manifesto* (New York: Cambridge University Press, 1960), and Clarence N. Stone, *Regime Politics: Governing of Atlanta, 1946–1988* (Lawrence: University Press of Kansas, 1989).

driven by U.S. oil interests and the importance of oil to the U.S. economy, as a whole, or the personal, economic interests of the American political elite, in particular. Perhaps the most important and influential economic determinist comes from Political Theory—Karl Marx—but please be aware that *not* all members of this school are Marxists.[10]

A third generic perspective is what I call the Power approach. In this perspective, political actors are also conceived to be rational, but rather than responding to the rules of the political game or the economy, they react to raw power.[11] Of course, in the varied realms of politics and policy, power can be many different things—people, natural resources, wealth, or military strength, for instance. But the arguments here all show that actors are motivated by power to minimize the costs of action and maximize the benefits. The Power approach is most notably used in international politics, where some scholars contend, for instance, that peace came to Europe after 1945 because power was relatively balanced there and nuclear weapons made conflict so deadly. Neither the United States nor the USSR (nor any of their allies) could believe that they could easily win a war on that continent. In fact, war would be highly costly and the outcome uncertain. From 1945-1990, then, a European war was irrational, while prior to World War II, there were times when power was imbalanced and thus one state (for instance, Germany in 1939) believed it could fight and win control of the continent at a reasonable cost.[12] Scholars from other

---

[10]Marxists are one particular type of economic determinist, who contend that the capitalist system is essentially exploitive in nature and that this exploitation will bring about its demise. Marxists argue that the laws of capitalism lead to the creation of monopolies, the emiseration of ordinary, and the concentration of capital into the hands of the few. These results often mean for Marxists that those with extraordinary economic power—industrial or financial leaders—wield political power or that the wealthiest capitalist state may act to preserve the capitalist world system, even if that action might seem not to be in the short term best interest of the hegemon. Although arguing from a "statist" or realist approach, Stephen Krasner, *Defending the National Interest* (Princeton: Princeton University Press, 1978) does a good job explaining a Marxist perspective. Also see Immanuel Wallerstein, *The Capitalist World Economy* (New York: Cambridge University Press, 1979) and Simon Clarke, Peter Fairbrother, Michael Burawoy, and Pavel Krotov, *What About the Workers? Workers and the Transition to Capitalism in Russia* (New York: Verso, 1993).

[11]Again, IR specialists have their own names for this group of scholars—realists or neo-realists.

[12]International relations specialists root this school of thought in the work of Thucydides. More modern examples of balance of power thinking are Hans Morgenthau and Kenneth W. Thompson, *Politics Among Nations: The Struggle for Power and Peace*, 6th ed (New York: Alfred A. Knopf, 1985), Kenneth Waltz, "Origins of War in Neorealist Theory," *Journal of Interdisciplinary History* 18, no. 4 (1988): 39–52, and John J. Mearsheimer "Back to the Future: Instability in Europe after the Cold War," *International Security* 15, no. 1 (Summer 1990), 5–56.

subfields have applied the notion of power (both explicitly and implicitly) to their own work. Notably, students of ethnic conflict look at the balance of strength (often defined demographically, geographically, institutionally, or economically) among ethnicities within societies to understand whether a divided society can ever become a stable one.[13] Students of labor relations, too, examine the way power is dispersed within the firm, the sector, and the whole economy to understand the potential for workers to affect conditions in their enterprises.[14] In Political Theory there is obviously a long tradition of studying power (providing the roots for the modern approach in international politics) dating back to Thucydides, Machiavelli, and Hobbes, to mention a few.

A fourth and final school is the "Culturalist" perspective. In opposition to institutionalists and power adherents, culturalists contend that there are, in essence, deeper sets of rules and norms (than those that flow from institutions or the distribution of strength) that govern and guide an actor's behavior. These conventions can be at the level of a national, regional, or local culture (e.g. that's the way—fill in the blank: Russians, Sicilians, New Yorkers—are). In other words, culture can reflect geographic and often temporal space and the ways of life of the people of that place and time. But it can also be specific to a "type" of people—i.e. within certain organizations, professions, generations, ethnicities, and genders. Some students of culture also contend that it more broadly reflects a set of behaviors and conventions that have defined "normal" interactions between players—states, ethnic groups, interest groups, or individuals.

Within the cultural school there is a divide between those that see culture as primordial (original or unchanging), and those that conceive of it as constructed or the product of interaction and interpretation.[15] This second sub-group, the constructivists, contends that material factors (like economic or power resources) as well as culture itself are not simply and objectively understood, but are interpreted through each agent's lenses. That is, resources and traditions are construed by an actor's

---

[13]For examples of balance of power thinking in Comparative Politics, see Chaim Kaufman, "Possible and Impossible Solutions to Ethnic Civil Wars," *International Security* 29 (Spring 1996), 136–175 and Steven L. Burg and Paul S. Shoup, *The War in Bosnia-Herzegovina: Ethnic Conflict and International Intervention* (Armonk, NY: M.E. Sharpe, 2000).

[14]Samuel B. Bacharach and Edward J. Lawler, *Bargaining: Power, Tactics, and Outcomes* (Washington, DC: Jossey-Bass Publishers, 1981).

[15]For one example of this contrast, see Samuel P. Huntington, "The Clash of Civilizations?" *Foreign Affairs* 72 (Summer 1993): 22–49, as a representative of the "primordial" perspective and John R. Bowen, "The Myth of Global Ethnic Conflict," *Journal of Democracy* 7, no. 4 (1996): 3–14 from the constructivist.

understanding of a situation and the practices that define the interactions of parties. Thus, resources as well as culture affect behavior. Finally, what distinguishes the constructivist subset from the primordialists as well as from the members of other schools is their contention that the participants in politics reinforce and at times transform the laws governing the interaction as well as the game itself by playing it. The rules are not simply set from the outset—by institutions or material factors—but are part of a system that is developed and sustained through the practices, knowledge, and resources of the players.[16]

Examples of culturalist explanations include those that argue that the political culture of different American cities affects the extent to which the benefits of downtown development are shared metropolis-wide.[17] In Comparative Politics, culturalists have argued that the norms and conventions of a region determine the extent to which democracy can flourish there. Places in which norms of reciprocity are deeply embedded are more likely to sustain democracy than those in which typical behavior reflects a twisted version of the "Golden Rule"—"Do unto others, before they have a chance to do harm to you!"[18] In International Politics, culturalists have argued that states are threatened not because another possesses nuclear weapons, but when that other is considered an enemy and develops WMD. Thus, the United States has never feared the British nuclear arsenal, but is extremely concerned about the North Korean one.[19]

Knowing that these generic approaches exist will help you when you start to read scholarly answers to your questions. You will be more easily able to categorize the different answers into schools of thought, although you should use more *specific* or *appropriate* (whether to your question or your sub-field) *labels* for your schools. If these are well-known schools, then use the established labels. If not, develop your own.

---

[16]In his influential formulation, Alexander Wendt noted that the realism and institutionalism "share a commitment to rationalism." In other words, they contend that external structures determine the interests as well as the identities—for example, rival, partner, rogue, or revisionist—and they miss the feedback between the behavior of the actors and who they are and what they desire. Alexander Wendt, "Anarchy Is What States Make of It: The Social Construction of Power Politics," *International Organization* 46, no. 2 (1992): 391–425.

[17]Stephen J. McGovern, *The Politics of Downtown Development: Dynamic Political Cultures in San Francisco and Washington, DC* (Lexington: University Press of Kentucky, 1999).

[18]Robert D. Putnam with Robert Leonardi and Raffaella Y. Nanetti, *Making Democracy Work: Civic Traditions in Modern Italy* (Princeton, NJ: Princeton University Press, 1993).

[19]Alexander Wendt, "Constructing International Politics," *International Security* 20, no. 1 (Summer 1995): 73–74.

USE THE RESOURCES YOU HAVE

As you begin investigating the literature on your question you should recognize an important fact: You probably have significant information and resources about your question close at hand. After all, you have taken at least one course on a related topic (your introductory class), and you may even have had an intermediate or advanced course on it. Your previous coursework can help you think about schools of thought and identify the most important approaches and scholars for your literature review.

Let's imagine that Diana, the third student that we met in the last chapter, is interested in studying something about nuclear proliferation. As she proceeds to define her research question, Diana decides that what most puzzles her is why the United States went to war with Iraq in March 2003 when its WMD programs were less advanced than those of other rogue states (namely Iran and North Korea). Although she is primarily concerned with a particular case—the 2003 U.S.-led war against Iraq—Diana's general question is "why do wars occur?" Any student of international politics should be able to reach into a toolkit (developed in the introductory class) and pull out a number of different theories. Perhaps my previous discussion of the generic schools of thought helped remind you of the "big ones" in international politics: realism, liberalism or idealism, Marxism, and constructivism. If you don't remember what you learned in your Introduction to International Politics (shame on you!), you can pull out your books and your notes from the course for help.

Using one of the most respected introductory texts, *World Politics: Trend and Transformation*, 9th ed. by Charles W. Kegley Jr. and Eugene R. Wittkopf, you can see that your first class in this subfield can provide you with a lot of guidance. If you look under "war" in the index, you might be overwhelmed. There are more than 30 subheadings. But if you turn to the Table of Contents, you can see that Chapter 2 might be a good place to start. It is called "Theories of World Politics" and it develops and assesses (as noted in the Table of Contents) liberalism, realism, neo-realism, neo-liberalism, and constructivism.[20] Thus, it provides you with an excellent summary of the major schools of thought in International Relations. You can use this to help you better answer your question about the causes of war, but—and this is a very

---

[20] *World Politics: Trend and Transformation*, 9th ed. (Belmont, CA: Wadsworth/Thomson Learning, 2004): 29–57. While I'm turning to Kegley and Wittkopf, I am confident that you could do the same with your own introductory text.

important caveat—just basing your understanding of the schools of thought on what you learn from your textbook is insufficient. To do an excellent job, you need to go to the work of the key scholars and see what they have to say *in their own words* on the causes of war. How do you find these important academics? They will be the people that the textbook authors mention by name or whose work is cited. So, you use the textbook to identify scholars and their particular works that you should consult. Moreover, because many of those works will be difficult to understand, reading your introductory text beforehand is an excellent way to be able to get the main ideas without struggling too hard.

Now, your textbook is likely to mention far more sources than you need to read. However, if you go back to your notes or any other readings that you had for the class, and start looking for the names of the most important authors, you could identify a subset of "must-reads." Given your knowledge and the help of the text, you might come up with this list:[21]

Liberalism:	Michael Doyle, *Ways of War and Peace* (New York: Norton, 1997).
Realism:	E.H. Carr, *The Twenty Years' Crisis, 1919–1939* (London: Macmillan, 1939).
	Hans J. Morgenthau, *Politics among Nations*, 6th ed. Revised by Kenneth W. Thompson. (New York: Knopf, 1985).
Neo-Realism:	Kenneth Waltz, *Theory of International Politics* (Reading, MA: Addison-Wesley, 1979).
Neo-liberalism:	Robert Keohane and Joseph S. Nye, *Power and Interdependence*, 3rd ed. (New York: Addison Wesley-Longman, 2001)
	Hedley Bull, *The Anarchical Society: A Study of Order in World Politics* (New York: Columbia University Press, 1977)
Constructivism:	Alexander Wendt, *Social Theory of International Politics* (New York: Cambridge University Press, 2000)

---

[21] *Ibid.* Please note: Kegley and Wittkopf provide all these names and the labels for you. Other introductory texts will do the same.

The textbooks often identify these authors' "big books," and the introductory and "theory" chapters of those works will be very helpful to you at this stage. Also, you can find a shorter statement of their ideas in an article. Then, you can locate these materials by consulting your library's online catalog or one of the databases. Each of these authors will have numerous books and articles; pick the one that you have seen cited or one that seems the most worthwhile to you by its title, abstract, and publication date. Other help in locating the "best" one for you can be found in your syllabi and bibliographies of the books used in your courses.

You might be thinking that finding schools of thought isn't so difficult after all. Here, I must be honest: of all the sub-fields, International Politics has been the most explicit in defining the schools of thought and using them to teach the introductory course. However, this doesn't mean that you can't find different perspectives in the other fields. For instance, looking at a very popular text in Comparative Politics, Thomas M. Magstadt's *Nations and Governments: Comparative Politics in Regional Perspective*, 5th ed., [22] you can find some clues. A quick perusal of its Table of Contents shows you that Magstadt identifies three key questions in the sub-field, two of which should sound familiar to you:

1. "Political Setting: How Do Unique Factors such as Environment, Culture, and History Influence Politics in Different Countries and Regions?

2. Patterns of Rule: How and Why Do Political Institutions, Patterns, and Trends Vary from One Region of the World to Another and What Forces Drive Change?"[23]

Hopefully, you can see that these two questions lead you to culturalist and institutionalist answers. Not surprisingly, as you read the text, you will see Magstadt highlighting the roles of cultures and institutions. And you can use his "Suggestions for Further Reading" at the end of each chapter to help you identify important and useful works.

Also remember that in your introductory classes you likely had, in addition to your text, readings for the course that dealt with specific and important issues. Often, these contain explanations and arguments and may be directly related to your research topic. Your professor also

---

[22]Published by Wadsworth/Thomson of Belmont, CA in 2005.

[23]Magstadt, ix.

might have given lectures related to your current project. So, be sure to go back and look at all the materials that you have from your classes and use them to help you.

PERFORM A SEARCH

At this point you are ready to consult the many resources that your library has to offer to find excellent sources for your literature review. Perhaps your job is very easy: Maybe you can consult a reader or collection of theoretical works to develop your literature review. Or you may have a list of citations from your courses and your textbook research and all you need to do is look them up in the library catalog or a database. But suppose you don't have any references (author names or actual citations) to work from. What do you do then?

First, you want to be sure to think about the topic in general. If you can't determine a general concept that captures the issue in which you are interested, go back to your textbook and read the title headings of the chapters. Which one looks appropriate for learning more about your topic? Hopefully, the title of that chapter will lead you to a concept that you can use to design your search. If not, look in the text of that chapter for words in boldface or at the end where key concepts are often listed. One or more of these terms should work for you as search words.

Second, before you start your search, sit down and think for a while. Consider the institutionalist, economic determinist, power, and culturalist explanations. Can you, on you own, develop answers to your question that follow from each of these perspectives? If you can spin these out, you will have an easier time recognizing them when you read them. Also, by thinking about schools of thought before you start your search you will be more ready both to understand different arguments when you see them and continue searching for alternative perspectives even after you have found one or two "good" articles.

Now you are ready to start your search. Where should you search? For most students, the answer is easy. They get on the Internet and "Google" the term. *Do not perform an Internet search at this stage.* While there are many useful sites on the Internet and you can find important information there, you do not want to collect articles for your literature review from it. Many people and organizations post information on the web, and at this stage, you have no idea how to determine whether these individuals are experts or quacks. Remember: the purpose of the literature review section is to explain and assess the *academic* debate. To find it, you need to turn to scholarly books and journals. As I recommended before, you should turn to your library's online catalog, Academic Search Premier, JSTOR, ProQuest or similar databases, where you can search the premier journals in Political Science.

As you begin searching, you may have some terms, authors (perhaps you identified the "big names" in the field from your course work), or even some seminal works. Start by looking for materials about which you have the most information. So, if you have the full citation for an article by Alexander Wendt, use all that information to pull up that very piece. As you find it, notice the subject searching terms that are listed when the article appears. Record these terms because you can use them to find related articles that likely will represent other perspectives on this topic.

If you do not have such detailed information or even an author's name, you want to search by subject or keyword using the terminology that you developed. Look for the most recent materials first. Then you have to look through your list. If you have more than 30 books and/or articles, narrow your search, either by combining terms or by introducing details about your case. If you're still having trouble, look for an article published in prestigious but more accessible journals such as the *Journal of Politics, Perspectives on Politics, PS: Political Science and Politics, Social Policy, Political Theory, Comparative Politics, Current History, Foreign Affairs, International Security,* and *World Politics.*[24] (Because reading scholarly articles is an art in itself, please see Box 3.1 for advice on effectively and efficiently reading such works. You should be able to use these tips for any reading that you do.)

In reading these sources, remember that scholars will use a format for their book or article similar to what I have recommended to you. So, you should be able to find their literature review section and discover how each author divides the field into schools of thought.[25] An author will also tell you who are the most important proponents of

---

[24]The *American Political Science Review* is also an excellent source. Because many of its articles use quantitative methods, I did not list it here as a good starting place for most new students of research.

[25]Sometimes, you can find an article that is solely a literature review. These will be very helpful in understanding the different approaches to your research question. Still, you should not copy or reiterate all of that author's analysis. You must think through the literature on your own. A great place for finding articles that summarize a field of inquiry is Ira Katznelson and Helen V. Milner, eds. *Political Science: State of the Discipline*, Centennial Edition (New York: W.W. Norton, 2005).

each view and what the essential works to read are. Thus, once you read a literature review, you are on your way to unlocking the scholarly debate on your question and finding other excellent sources for you to consult for your own paper. You still must use care, however, not to accept someone else's assessment of the field on face value. Each author has a particular argument that he is making, and while you may agree with it, you cannot be sure until after you have read other principal works too. Thus, you should read a few different scholarly works or literature review sections carefully to help you have an idea of the debate and the major players in it. After taking careful notes (see Box 3.1 for specific advice), you are in the position to write your own literature review. You now know how the field is divided, and you can place the most important authors into different groups.

WRITING THE LITERATURE REVIEW

The literature review answers the following questions:

1. How have important scholars answered my general research question? What are the most important schools of thought and who are identified with them? What is an appropriate label for this group of authors? Why?

2. What are the strengths (logical or explanatory) of each school of thought? What are the weaknesses?

3. In conclusion, which school of thought seems the best?

Your notes on your reading (see Box 3.1) have been directed at helping you answer precisely these questions. It is now time for you to transform them into an essay. As with any section of this paper, you should think of the literature review both as a stand-alone essay—with a purpose all its own—and as a part of the greater whole. Thus, you need to develop a title, as well as an introduction, body, and conclusion for this "essay" or section of your paper. The title will become a heading (if it *were* an independent essay, you would put the title on a separate page with your name, date, and course information).

What is a good title for a literature review? You may think, "'Literature Review,' that's perfect." Well, ask yourself, as you were reading the scholarly works did you see many published authors who used that title in their paper? Typically, authors use more informative headings, just like you would use a more specific title than simply "Essay 1" for the first essay that you wrote for one of your classes. You must come

---

B O X 3.1 How to Read and Take Notes on Articles and Books

Scholarly articles and books can be very difficult to read, but you need to learn to do so in order to use these materials in your research project. As you approach this task, you should remember that scholars tend to follow the same basic outline for their research papers that you are being exposed to now. Understanding that papers or books are written in sections or chapters that typically perform the same basic tasks is a useful key to unlocking part of the meaning of these works. The rest you will have to discern for yourself. Below, I have some advice for reading and taking notes so that you will more quickly and accurately understand academic authors. Please note: This advice can help you with any reading that you have to do for your courses, not just your reading for your research paper.

Step 1   *CHECK IT OUT:* First, look at the piece and try to determine its logical structure by reading and thinking about the **subject headings** in the text. These headings are the author's outline, so they give you a key to the plan of the essay. Can you identify the introductory, literature review, methods, analysis, and concluding sections? After you finish reading and thinking about the headings, read the introductory and concluding sections. DO NOT TAKE NOTES UNTIL AFTER YOU HAVE READ BOTH. When you finish, you should be able to write down the author's argument (also called a thesis). If the thesis is not clear, reread the conclusion until you can identify it. Now, you are ready to begin reading the text. The rest of the article will provide the logic and evidence that led the author to conclude with that thesis.

Step 2   *MARK IT UP/LOOK IT UP:* Go back to the beginning and read the text carefully, with the goal of identifying the argument and the evidence that the author provides to support the thesis. As you read, mark the text and make brief notes in the margins near any important, interesting, or confusing items. Try to mark where the author provides the argument and gives evidence to support the thesis. Also, have a dictionary handy so that you can look up words that are unfamiliar to you. DO NOT simply skip over words that you do not know. If you do not know the meaning of the words the author uses, can you really expect to understand the argument? In your notebook, write down the definitions of the words that you look up and learn them. If the dictionary doesn't seem to provide a good definition (perhaps because the term is one specific to political science), look up this word in the glossary of the appropriate introductory text.

Step 3   *WRITE IT DOWN:* After you have finished reading the article, you can go back and take notes. Your job is to identify the author's argument (double check your work in Step 1 above) as well as to determine the logic and evidence that the author provides to sustain his reasoning. Go back to the marks in the text, and write down material that provides insight into the author's reasoning and the facts that he cites to support his thesis. Also, be sure to look again at the passages of which you were unsure initially. Do you understand them now? If not, try to write down in your notes exactly what is not clear to you.

Step 4 CRITIQUE IT: Now think critically about what you have read and recorded. Is the author's argument logical? For instance, is it plausible that the identified cause could lead to the particular phenomenon in question? Then look at the evidence that the author supplies. Does that evidence really support his claim? Is the author using the facts properly or has he slanted them to help make the case? In addition, can you think of other facts that the author does not include that will discredit the argument? Can you think of a similar instance that will not fit? Jot down any problems that you can see with the author's argument, the use of evidence, or the application of this approach to a comparable case. Or, more positively, does the author's argument seem to apply to other similar cases? Has he used evidence carefully? Why is this piece so good?

Step 5 RELATE IT: Finally, relate this piece to other works that you have read. What type of an argument is the author making? (In other words, in what school of thought or family of theories would this piece belong?) To which works is this piece similar? Different? Why?

If you follow the guidelines specified here, your notes on your readings will look like the following (Please note that you may NOT always be able to fill in something for each part. For instance, you might not find any logical or evidentiary problems or the author might not use any terms with which you are not familiar. But, you should always identify the thesis, logic, evidence, and the work's links to other things you have read.)

Vocabulary:
Thesis:
Logic:
Evidence:
Cases other than the ones you want to study for which this argument makes sense:
Critique:
    Logical problems:
    Evidentiary problems:
    Other cases for which this argument does not make sense:
Relationship to other works you have read:
    In what school of thought or theoretical "family" does this piece belong?
    To which works does it seem most similar? Why?
    To which works does it seem most opposed? Why?

up with a good section title for your literature review. If you keep in mind the purpose of the section—understanding and assessing the scholarly debate on your research question—then naming it isn't so hard. The focus is on your question and the multiple answers to it. Suppose Latisha, our student who wants to run for office, was trying to understand why the party in power, the Republicans, did so well in the 2002 off-year elections. The following titles are examples of good ones for a literature review on that topic: "Who Wins in Off-Year Elections: Three Perspectives," "Different Views on Off-Year Elections," or "Understanding the Outcomes of Off-Year Elections." Each heading highlights the general topic (off-year election results) and suggests that Latisha will be looking at several explanations.

After the title, you need to provide an introduction to the section that explains to the reader that there is a scholarly debate on your research question, there are roughly "X" number of schools focusing on these specific factors, but that one school seems to be the best one. Then, in the body of the section, you lay out each of the perspectives, assess them, and write a conclusion that defends your preference.

I can't stress enough that *a literature review is not simply a set of paragraph book or article summaries of three or four different authors.* Instead, a literature review tells the reader "I understand the debate in the field. I can explain different answers to my general research question that follow from the most important perspectives in the discipline. Here are the logical strengths and weaknesses of the answers, and because one approach seems most compelling, I like it best." (Of course, your essay best accomplishes these goals without actually using the word "I" or stating these points in a colloquial manner.)

There are several ways of organizing a literature review. One is to present the approaches in chronological order, as a means of showing the historical development of an area of inquiry. Another is to mention and discuss the schools from the least to the most preferred. Choose the order that best works to highlight the debate and makes your tasks (of introducing the general question, the various arguments, and your preferred position) easiest for you.

When you are first setting out a perspective, you should present a school in its most favorable light. After you explain an approach, you can assess it critically, particularly with respect to its logic and explanatory power (for cases other than the ones you want to study). Please, however, do not mix the analysis with the exposition.

Remember Matt from Chapter 2? He was the student that came to Political Science because of his interests in the 2000 and 2004 elections. Well, he ultimately decided to investigate whether the United States should use the Electoral College to choose the president. Below is an excerpt of a literature review that he wrote for a paper entitled "The Electoral College: Necessity or Anachronism?"[26] I have included here the introductory paragraph from this section of his paper and the elucidation of his fourth school of thought. While the whole section also included discussions of three other schools and a concluding paragraph that justified precisely why he preferred the "Federalist" view, this excerpt provides you with a good example of a section introduction and an exposition of one school's answer to his research question.

THE LITERATURE ON THE ELECTORAL COLLEGE

The debate over the Electoral College and its role as a modern political institution is not new. The discussion involves not only this institution, but the fundamental aspects of the American political system. Scholars who write about the College may be divided into analytical categories: those who seek to discover the original intent of the Framers and those who try to understand the logic of the Constitution and its modern application. From these two groupings come four general schools of thought on whether the Electoral College remains useful for and consistent with American democracy today: Traditionalism, Pragmatism, Nationalism and Federalism. Traditionalism and Pragmatism are unconvincing. The Traditionalists are too simplistic, and the Pragmatist argument is more an excuse than a reasoned response. The debate between the Nationalists and Federalists is compelling, however. The Nationalists find the College problematic because it distorts democracy. The Federalists, on the other hand, claim that this method of selection provides the appropriate balance (found in other areas of the U.S. Constitution) between individual and states' rights. . . .

[Skipping to the exposition of the fourth school of thought. . .]

The Federalist argument strikes at the heart of the Electoral College debate. The concept of equality among states, and the primacy of their power is one of the core principles on which the nation and the Electoral College are founded. Indeed, the Tenth Amendment provides that all powers not delegated to the federal government, or prohibited from the states by

---

[26]Included by permission of the author, unpublished draft ms., Saint Joseph's University, April 2005.

the Constitution, are reserved for the states.[27] Federalism not only provides power to the states, but it is also a check on the authority of the national government. Madison stated that the goal of federalism was to divide and arrange the several offices in such a manner as that each may be a check on the other. . . .These inventions of prudence cannot be less requisite in the distribution of the supreme powers of the State.[28]

Decades later, John C. Calhoun made a similar argument in his "A Disquisition on Government." He wrote that government has its origin in society and the individual; government is instituted to protect society and the individuals that inhabit it. In discussing what should constitute a government, Calhoun also sought to dispel a myth: "The first and leading error which naturally arises from overlooking the distinction referred to is to confound the numerical majority with the people, and this is so completely as to regard them as identical."[29] States are prime in the government, and they, not the citizens, ought to have equality in their representation.

However, before one goes off on a tirade that this institution is undemocratic, let it be admitted that it *is* undemocratic, but very republican. Judith A. Best, a proponent of the Electoral College and the author of *The Choice of the People?*, constructs her argument for the Electoral College on the principle of federalism. She claims that because representation in the federal government is built on two constitutional principles—state equality and federal districting—the presidency must be found in that juxtaposition. Furthermore, she states that "in a large, heterogeneous, continental republic there must be a balance between the local and the national interests so that the legitimate interests of the people in one part of the whole nation are not carelessly neglected or unnecessarily sacrificed. There must be a way to protect the interests of the local minority."[30] That is not to say that citizens have no rights, but their rights are

---

[27]"Constitution of the United States, Amendment 10," in *The Federalist Papers*, ed. Clinton Rossiter (New York: The New American Library of World Literature, 1961, p. 544.

[28]James Madison, "Federalist 51," in *The Federalist Papers*, ed. Clinton Rossiter (New York: The New American Library of World Literature, 1961), p. 322.

[29]John C. Calhoun, "A Disquisition of Government," in *American Political Thought*, 5th ed., ed. Kenneth M. Dolbeare and Michael S. Cummings (Washington, DC: Congressional Quarterly, 2004), pp. 213-14, 220.

[30]Judith A. Best, *The Choice of the People? Debating the Electoral College* (Lanham, MD: Rowman & Littlefield Publishers, 1996), p. 32, 34

framed in the context of the states, and the states' rights are framed under an agreement known as the U.S. Constitution. Alexander Bickel in *Reform and Continuity* says that a major flaw in the electoral system, the perceived disenfranchisement of the individual voter, is also the source of its greatest wisdom: "The genius of the present system is the genius of a popular democracy organized on the federal principle, and much is to be gained from it in a country as large and still as diverse as ours." Bickel notes that the Electoral College and the makeup of the Senate symbolically reflect the fairness and equality of the states in the nation. They give hope and aspiration to small states and serve the needs of large ones. [31]

Notice some of the strengths of this excerpt of Matt's literature review. His introduction to the section is very strong. In it, he tells the reader that there are four schools of thought, gives each a descriptive label, communicates which schools are more interesting, and explains the basic arguments of these two approaches. Perhaps he could have more clearly set out the arguments of the other two or told the reader which one he ultimately preferred, but Matt knew he had the body of the Literature Review to explain each approach and he could be relying on convention for communicating his preferences. He may think that we know he favored the Federalist argument because he discussed it last. Another improvement to the introduction might be to restate the precise research question. Otherwise readers might be unsure of the exact parameters of the Electoral College debate. Lastly, perhaps Matt could develop a better title for his section. What heading would accurately capture what he is doing here?

In explaining the fourth school, Matt does an excellent job. Now notice what Matt doesn't do: He doesn't summarize a single (or even several) books or articles. Instead, he answers his research question by identifying key concepts and turning to classics in American political thought to assert the importance of these ideas and to explicate their meaning. Guess where he was likely exposed to those works? Probably he read Federalist 51 in his introductory American Government course, or perhaps he read that and Calhoun's piece in another class, American Political Thought. Thus, Matt is using the work he has done in other courses to inform and improve the paper that he writes here. Because he is seeking to cumulate the knowledge developed over the course of his academic career, Matt's paper is actually easier

---

[31] Alexander Bickel, *Reform and Continuity: The Electoral College, The Convention, and The Party System* (New York: Harper & Row, 1971), p. 14, 10.

to write (he's already read and thought about these pieces) and better (he demonstrates a broad grounding in American politics).

Then, Matt moves on to discuss two important *books*[32] that address this debate. Here, Matt shows his reader that he has done outside research and that he has found good sources. Using Best and Bickel, Matt explains further the importance of states in American democracy and suggests that the College better reflects American political traditions than does simple majoritarianism. Fabulous work, Matt!

PROPERLY DOCUMENTING YOUR LITERATURE REVIEW (AND ALL OF YOUR WORK IN YOUR RESEARCH PAPER)

Proper documentation (providing citations to the works that have helped you formulate your ideas and supplied information) is essential in a research paper. You should be prepared from the beginning of the writing process to be keeping track of the sources that you use and the precise places in the text that these authors have influenced your work. That means that you must choose a particular format, such as the MLA (Modern Language Association), APA (American Psychological Association), or *Chicago* (*Chicago Manual of Style*) form. In Political Science, any of these formats are acceptable, but your professor may have a preference for one in particular. So, you need to learn to follow that form. I prefer the *Chicago Manual of Style* because it uses formal footnotes or endnotes (not simply in-text citations). Moreover, several of the premier journals in my subfield—International Relations—tend to use this format. Thus, you will see the *Chicago* style in this book. No matter what form you choose, however, be consistent and follow it precisely. Get a style manual to consult; you do not have to memorize the format, but you should not make up your own style as you go along.

Once you have chosen a format for documentation, you need to keep careful track of where and how different works influence you. First, I recommend that you open a new document and begin to work on your bibliography from the time you start writing your first

---

[32]I am not asserting that books are always better than articles, but students tend to overuse the Internet (even overusing good online databases) in search of journal articles and miss out on important works. Thus, I wanted to draw your attention here to Matt's use of books.

draft.[33] That way, you won't have to type all of your sources in when you are frantically trying to finish. Also, you won't lose any citations and have to look them up again. Finally, in *Chicago Manual of Style* you can use the bibliographic cite for your footnotes, with some modification.[34]

As you write the text of your paper, you also need to keep track of the precise places in your work where you benefited from both the ideas and the exact words of your sources. You might be surprised to learn that you need to give credit for ideas and not simply quotes and figures. This point is so important, I'll repeat it: *No matter what citation form you choose, you must attribute ideas to their original author.* Moreover, you should avoid using direct quotes too frequently in your text. Your paper is supposed to be your view of a particular issue, so you need to put other authors' ideas into your own words. If you do not, then you are plagiarizing. Plagiarism is an extremely serious academic offense, the equivalent of a scholarly crime. The plagiarist steals another's prized possession: his thoughts and hard work, and passes them off as her own.[35] Most institutions of higher learning punish plagiarists severely, putting them on academic probation or throwing them out of school. Once you have been identified as a plagiarist, you can often forget about postgraduate education, especially law school. The lesson: *never plagiarize, neither intentionally nor accidentally.* Keep careful track of the works that have contributed to your intellectual development, and learn how to cite and paraphrase properly.

While one way to avoid plagiarism is to provide complete quotes (properly cited) from your sources throughout your paper, this approach is not the most effective. Think back to some of the works that you have already read in preparation for writing your literature review. How many of them contained a copious number of direct quotes? I would venture to guess that none did. Your goal, then, is to minimize direct quotes, but maintain, even maximize, the footnotes. Of course you must be sure to mention the author's name in your text so as to associate him with the ideas, but you need to find your own formulation. Making your version different enough from the author's can be difficult, especially if you have the work open in front of you and/or you are trying to capture the sense of a particular sentence (a small amount of text).

---

[33]I am using the *Chicago Style* term here (and will continue to do so throughout) for the list of works that you consulted in your project. MLA calls this "Works Cited," and for APA it's "References." For all, the works are listed in alphabetical order by author last name. It is NOT numbered. Each approach treats the entries slightly differently, so consult a manual for the precise format.

[34]In-text citations for MLA and APA are much less involved.

[35]Thanks to Mary Frances Malone for this formulation.

B O X 3.2 Paraphrasing and Plagiarism: Knowing the Difference

---

Immediately below is an excerpt from John Lewis Gaddis, *We Now Know: Rethinking Cold War History* (New York: Oxford University Press, 1997), pp. 87–88. After that, I've provided examples of paraphrasing and plagiarism, documented in the MLA form. Can you tell which is which?

Original Source:

> Nuclear weapons were developed in a traditional way, but in an untraditional place. The way was traditional because scientific advances—particularly the discovery of atomic fission in the late 1930s—coincided with an opportunity to use them, which was the onset of World War II; it was not the first time the prospect of a war had stimulated the development of technologies with which to fight it. The place, though, was unexpected. Despite its impressive industrial capabilities and deeply-rooted military traditions, the United States through most of its history had hardly led the world in developing new warfighting technologies. Americans had tended to imitate rather than to originate weaponry, and during the 1920s and 1930s they barely managed to maintain functional professional forces at any level. The army he commanded was still training with horses and mules when in October 1941 the President of the United States authorized a crash program, in collaboration with British and Canadian allies, to produce an atomic bomb.

1. According to John Lewis Gaddis, nuclear weapons were developed in a typical way, but in an unusual location. The way was typical because science and its applications occurred at the same time that a war started (87–88).

My recommendation is that you close the book or journal, and not look at it as you try to express these ideas in your own words. You will also have an easier time avoiding plagiarism if you are distilling a larger chunk of text into a smaller one. If you're trying to condense a chapter into one paragraph, you simply cannot use the precise words in the chapter. *Do not* consult any summary paragraph you may find in the introduction or conclusion of the book or article; you will run a grave risk of plagiarizing by not making your text significantly different enough from the author's. Box 3.2 provides some insight into proper paraphrasing and plagiarism.[36]

The bottom line here is to use your own words, but still give the author credit. It was his idea, and your reader is likely to know that.

---

[36]See Diana Hacker, *A Pocket Manual of Style*, 4th ed. (Boston: Bedford/St. Martin's, 2004), pp. 115–126, 157–164, 185–192

2. John Lewis Gaddis contends that the American development of nuclear weapons in the 1940s was in some ways usual and unusual. As
usual, engineers and scientists in that decade found a real-world
application for the theoretical discovery of fission. Atypically, however, the United States, along with Great Britain and Canada, was the
site of this innovation. In the past, other countries in the world had
been at the forefront of military technology, while the United States
was a follower. This time, however, the United States took the lead
(Gaddis 87–88).

3. Americans tended to copy rather than to invent new armaments, and
during the interwar period they barely managed to keep professional
forces at a functional level.

Answers:

1. Plagiarism. Although the author and page numbers are provided, the
student uses Gaddis' first eight words verbatim. In the rest, the
sentence construction and language are far too close to Gaddis'.

2. Paraphrase. The student has captured the sense of the paragraph in
her own words. She gives the author credit in the citation and
provides the page numbers.

3. Plagiarism. The student uses the same sentence construction and
words very similar (with some synonyms) to Gaddis. In addition, the
student fails to give the author any credit (either in the text or with a
citation).

You will impress the reader by showing that you know the literature
and can express in your own words the ideas of this scholar. If you
find, however, that you simply cannot effectively communicate this
author's arguments in your own words, then use a direct quote. The
direct quote also requires its own footnote, of course. Whether
you've conveyed the ideas or used a direct quote, you need to include
in the citation the page number in the text from which either came.

PRACTICAL SUMMARY

In this chapter, you have learned how to write a literature review.
Central to this goal is finding the appropriate literature, identifying
the most important scholars involved in the debate, understanding

the different answers to the research question that these authors posit, and placing these scholars into different schools of thought by determining the key factors or underlying points that unite and divide them. You now know how and where to find academic authors, what some standard perspectives are, and how to make sense of debates. In addition, the chapter gave you a basic outline of your literature review, discussed the importance of and method for proper documentation of sources, and included an excerpt from Matt's literature review.

The steps to follow when you need to write the literature review are:

1. Identify the *general research question*.

2. Find the most important scholarly answers to date to that question by
   a. Consulting your books and notes from related classes to determine the principal authors and schools of thought.
   b. Thinking on your own about what some possible explanations from different schools of thought could be.
   c. Searching (with the help of steps (a) and (b) to identify authors and terms) the library catalog and premier journals in Political Science for important works.
   d. Reading these books and articles and taking careful notes (see advice in Box 3.1) with the specific goals of identifying (i) schools of thought, (ii) key authors, and (iii) works that you need to read.

3. Write a draft of your literature review. Recognize that it should be integrated into the whole paper, but also make sense as a stand-alone essay. Thus, the literature review section has its own introduction, body, and conclusion. This part of the paper can map into the following outline:
   I. How have important scholars answered my general research question? What are the most important schools of thought and who are identified with them? What is an appropriate label for this group of authors? Why?
      A. School 1
         1. Give it a label, and identify its logic and main adherents.
         2. How would this school answer the particular research question?
         3. What are its logical strengths and weaknesses?

    B. School 2
        1. Give it a label, and identify its logic and main adherents.
        2. How would this school answer the particular research question?
        3. What are its logical strengths and weaknesses?
    C. School 3 (assuming there are three schools, and continue this format if you have more than three schools)
        1. Give it a label, and identify its logic and main adherents.
        2. How would this school answer the particular research question?
        3. What are its logical strengths and weaknesses?

II. In conclusion, which school of thought seems to provide the best answer? Why?

4. Properly document the sources. You must give credit to any author who helped you understand the general layout of the field, and you must read and cite the major scholars participating in the debate. In the body of your literature review, each paragraph will have several footnotes in it, citing the authors and the works mentioned in the text. It is impossible to write a good literature review, free of plagiarism that lacks citations. This section is all about showing the reader that you know the literature, the major, written works on the topic.

5. Develop a heading or title for the literature review section. It should indicate that there is debate on your topic.

6. Keep in mind that this is *your perspective* on the literature. You should feel free to develop labels and take an unpopular position (as long as you can defend it!). The highly influential Political Scientist Theodore J. Lowi used to tell his graduate students, "Be bold!" That advice applies here.

7. Finally, be sure to conclude with what you believe is the strongest answer to the research question and convince the reader that you have made the best choice.

SUGGESTED CALENDAR

Follow your professor's instructions, but typically you will want to complete the first draft of your literature review at a relatively early stage of the course. Recognize that you may have to come back to it and rethink some elements or include more sources, but work to identify and label the key schools and highlight the most important factor(s) at this early time.

EXERCISES

1. Without doing any research, help Latisha with her research project. Use any three of the four generic schools (Institutionalism, Economic Determinism, the Power Approach, or Culturalism) to develop an answer to the following questions: Why do certain candidates in the United States get elected and others lose? Develop a title for the literature review section.

2. Think of a better title for the literature review section of Matt's paper on whether the Electoral College should be the arbiter of American presidential elections.

3. Determine three schools of thought in response to the following research question: Why does democracy function better in some places in the world than in others? Go through the following steps as you work on this question: (a) Consider the question on your own and try to jot down answers based on your knowledge of the generic schools of thought; (b) Consult your introductory Comparative Politics text, notes and other readings; (c) Use your library's online catalog to find some important books for this topic; and (d) Go to an online database via your library's website to search the prestige journals in political science. What have you found? What would you name the literature review section of a research paper considering this question?

4. Pick any research question of interest to you and go through the following steps to identify the scholarly debate: (a) Consider the question on your own and try to jot down answers based on your knowledge of the generic schools of thought; (b) Consult your introductory text, notes and other readings; (c) Consult your library's online catalog to find some important books for this topic, and (d) Use one of the online data bases to search the prestige journals in political science. What have you found? What would you name the literature review section of a research paper considering this question? Which school do you prefer? Why?

4

Effectively Distilling the Argument: The Thesis or the Model and Hypothesis

A s we proceed in this paper-writing marathon, finishing the Literature Review is like running the first eight miles. You've completed a little less than a third of the race, and you can see a long, slightly upward sloping stretch in front of you. But you are well trained and ready for this challenge. You will persevere by proceeding steadily and remembering that the parts of the paper are interrelated in ways that help you move from one phase to the next. The conclusion of the Literature Review leads the writer to a bottom line: One answer to the research question appears best. In effect, that conclusion is the fundamental **argument** or **thesis** that you will be sustaining, evaluating, or testing in your research paper.[1] For experienced writers, stating this conclusion in the Literature Review is often sufficient for guiding them through the rest of the process. For less experienced authors or for

---

[1]The thesis will also appear prominently in your Introduction, but since we haven't talked about that section yet, I did not mention the Introduction here.

particularly complex arguments, the **Model and Hypothesis** section is brief but important. It forces the author to state precisely what she expects to find. In an empirical paper, that statement will come in two forms—in a picture or flow diagram (**model**) and words (**hypothesis**).

THE THESIS

Almost all of the writing (except creative) that you do in college will have a thesis or an argument.[2] A thesis is a *contentious statement,* that is, a declaration or description with which reasonable people could disagree. A thesis can be either a normative claim or an empirically verifiable contention. Only some theses, however, identify a causal relationship or are primarily interested in the relationship between the factors under consideration.[3] Sometimes an author is more interested in exploring a surprising and sometimes counterintuitive point of fact.

You are used to reading works with theses, as you are exposed to them in the essays that you read for classes, Op-Ed pieces in newspapers, journals of opinion such as *The New Republic, The American Prospect, The Weekly Standard, The Nation,* and *The National Review,* or even some journals, particularly ones that minimize footnotes, may lack a bibliography, and are written for a more general audience (such as *Social Policy, Foreign Affairs, Current History,* or *Foreign Policy*).[4] Often, students think that developing and sustaining a thesis in this manner is the only way to write a research paper. It is not, as we will see, and in fact, many empirical political scientists prefer that your research question explore the **correlation** of **variables** or a *causal relationship* between factors.

We have already seen one example of a thesis. Remember Matt's paper? He claims that the Electoral College should continue to determine the outcome of American elections because it better reflects

---

[2]Throughout this work, I will use these two terms—argument and thesis—interchangeably. Two exceptions to the universal claim at the opening of this sentence include some types of journals and journalism.

[3]Thus, I am using "thesis" or "argument" in a broad sense. As we will see, I am defining a hypothesis as a type of thesis. In essence, "thesis" is the broad class, while hypothesis refers to a specific type.

[4]Please note that textbooks frequently do not have theses, instead describing the state of a field without taking a position that one approach is best. Of course, some texts do have an embedded thesis. Most famously, Hans Morgenthau's *Politics among Nations* is a text in international politics that puts forth a realist view of the field.

American political traditions than does a contest in which the candidate receiving the highest vote total wins. That assertion is certainly a contentious statement. Another possible thesis on very different topic, the role of the courts, could be: In the United States, the courts are not an effective instrument of social change. Again, many reasonable people would take issue with this assertion, because the courts, particularly in the second half of the twentieth century, played an important role in transforming American society.[5] Civil rights, women's, environmental and gay groups, for example, have all turned to the legal system to bring about changes that they could not otherwise achieve. Given the success of the Civil Rights movement's legal campaign culminating in *Brown v. Board of Education,* many have categorically accepted the importance of using the courts for social change. This thesis calls the conventional wisdom into question. Of course, the person who put forth this argument didn't arrive at it out of thin air. Instead, the thesis would have come from personal experience or reflection, class work, or readings on the courts and the transformation of American society. And while there may be a causal relationship (extent of the perceived legal "overreach" → extent of mobilization of citizens and groups opposed to change → level of actions taken to prevent or reverse change) that explains *why* the courts aren't that useful in remaking society, investigating the causality is not the central goal of a paper with this thesis. Instead, this student wants to evaluate the *utility* of the court as an instrument for social change.

Another thesis of this nature comes from International Politics: Hard-line leaders are more likely to succeed in achieving peace or rapprochement with enemies than are soft-liners. Again, there may be a causal connection (stability of a leader's domestic position → nature of the peace-making process, where hard-liners are politically less vulnerable to attacks that they are "soft" and so are more able to make concessions to enemies), but tracing the links between the variables is of less interest to the student. Instead, this researcher wants to investigate the *correlation* of events: the existence of hard-line leaders and the achievement of peace.

If causation means that one factor (a cause) brings about an effect, then correlation refers to instances when two or more factors change together. Adjustments in one factor necessarily occur *with* changes

---

[5]See for example Gerald Rosenberg, *The Hollow Hope: Can Courts Bring About Social Change?* (Chicago: University of Chicago Press, 1991) and Michael McCann, *Rights at Work: Pay Equity and the Politics of Legal Mobilization* (Chicago: University of Chicago Press, 1994).

in the other. With causation, the transformation of the first factor (the cause) must always precede an alteration in the second, the effect. If the chronology of events (change in the first bringing about change in second) is violated, then a researcher must doubt that he has found a causal relation. With correlation, the order in which the changes occur is not of importance. Rather, an analyst is interested in simply showing that these factors move together.

Not all theses explore a correlation, however. In fact, as we saw with Matt, many works in political theory, constitutional politics, or political development (among other fields), make a contentious statement about the meaning or intent of important thinkers or political documents.[6] For instance, in a 2001 piece in *The Journal of Politics,* Richard Boyd notes that students of Hobbes have often argued about whether he is "a defender of royalist absolutism . . . [or] the intellectual forefather of liberal individualism." Boyd asserts that the first interpretation is the proper one; Hobbes fears civil society groups and the chaos that they bring to politics. Instead, Hobbes prefers the order provided by a kingly sovereign, and is, therefore, *not* an early father of liberalism.[7]

Another example of this type of thesis—currently hotly debated as a result of Samuel P. Huntington's latest work *Who Are We?*—is that the Founders never intended to create an impenetrable barrier between Church and State. Instead, by prohibiting a state-sponsored religion, they were securing freedom *for* and not *from* religion in the new republic.[8] With both Boyd's and Huntington's theses, the authors are putting forth a statement that they believe is true. They seek to undermine other interpretations that disagree with their own. In their simplest forms the theses are, respectively,

- Hobbes is an opponent of liberal associationalism; he defends and supports royal rule.[9]

---

[6]I could also have noted the many works in comparative and international politics that stress the importance of intersubjective understandings and the development of meanings. As one example, see Paul Dixon, *Northern Ireland: The Politics of War and Peace* (New York: Palgrave, 2001).

[7]Richard Boyd, "Thomas Hobbes and the Perils of Pluralism," *The Journal of Politics* 63 (2001), pp. 392–413, quote from p. 392.

[8]While numerous scholars have written on this subject, Samuel Huntington's latest work has brought this issue to the forefront again. (And this is just one thesis of this form among several in this contentious book.) See Samuel P. Huntington, *Who Are We? The Challenges to America's National Identity* (New York: Simon & Schuster, 2004).

[9]Boyd.

- Religion was (and should continue to be) central to the formation of the American government and governance. The American identity is (and should continue to be) Protestant.[10]

Here the point is *not* to examine how certain factors are related to or affect each other but rather to validate some important *truth*.[11]

When the work is organized around a thesis, the primary goal of the research is often prescriptive, normative, and/or insightful. For the student of social change, it provides a set of lessons for how to achieve transformation. For the student of conflict, it might suggest how one ought to vote to bring about peace. And for the political theorist, investigating these contentions often provides a better understanding of what the great thinkers meant or how politics should be.

THE MODEL

While a thesis or argument is the broad term for the contention that you are investigating throughout your research, I will use another set of terms for work that is explicitly and self-consciously empirical. Empiricists explore correlations and causations, and seek to chart carefully the relationships between variables. Frequently, they use the language of science when engaging in their research and explaining it to others. In Chapter 2, we noted that empirical research seeks to explain a particular phenomenon or solve some puzzle. In its most basic form, an empirical argument can be reduced to relationships between **variables,** where a variable is anything that can vary, change in value. What you are trying to explain is the "effect" or the **dependent variable.** This effect "depends" on some other factors (the causes) and it is a variable because, if the value of the causes change, so too will the effect. The cause is referred to as the **independent variable.**[12]

Upon first consideration, thinking of concepts in Political Science as variables with values can be quite strange for students. Probably, you are used to thinking of variables as something that you find only in math class—"x" or "y"—and values bring up the idea of

---

[10]Huntington.

[11]Notice that Matt's argument is of the same type.

[12]Certainly, there can be multiple causes or several independent variables. For simplicity's sake, I will be talking about a single cause here. Also, technically, when first stated these are concepts and through operationalization, they become variables. See Chapter 6 for more on operationalization.

numbers. Most Political Science majors are attracted to this subject because they believe, among other things, that this discipline will be about words, not manipulating equations with numbers. But concepts in Political Science can be variables and take on values. In saying that they can be variables I am simply noting that they can change. Take for instance the concept "party identification." In the United States, there is more than one party, and people identify with different ones or have no attachment to parties at all. Thus, the values that the variable "party identification" can take on are "Republican, Democrat, Independent, Other, or None." While a large number of variables in Political Science cannot be measured in numbers, there are also many that can be quantified. Voter turnout, presidential popularity, educational outcomes, Supreme Court voting patterns, election results, and budget deficits are just a few examples. Given a particular time and place, these variables will take on different values.

In empirical research, literature reviews often divide the field into schools that identify one independent variable (causal factor) to be more important than others. Moreover, the research question asks about the dependent variable (effect). Thus, as a result of your literature review, you should be able to generate a number of independent variables that potentially have an impact on the phenomenon in which you are interested. In effect, by performing the literature review you have identified the information that you need to develop a number of competing models. A model is the pictorial representation of your argument or thesis, reducing it to its "bare bones," the basic elements that are related to each other.

You may wonder why you must develop a model if it follows so nicely from the literature review. Well, in one sense, the model is a check on your work; it makes sure that you have done the literature review correctly. Unfortunately, students sometimes use the literature review to discuss in very abstract terms the way that different schools of thought *conceive of politics* instead of focusing on how each perspective *answers the general research question* at hand. If you have done your literature review correctly, coming up with the variables will be easy. If you have improperly written this section, developing models will be very difficult. So, if you cannot develop a model, then you know that you need to go back and redo your literature review before you can proceed with your research.

Let's think back to Kate's research interests to look at the relationship between the literature review, variable identification, and models. Kate started out with a general interest in women, gender, and politics, but began zeroing in on the question of why women are more likely to be elected in some countries than in others. In writing her literature review, Kate decided that the question of electoral success of women was really related to the level of democracy that prevails in any society, reasoning that greater participation of women reflected a more open, democratic system. So, to answer her question about levels of female political empowerment, she turned to the literature that seeks to explain the levels of democracy in any society. She found that there were three basic explanations: (a) an institutional argument that claims that women are more likely to be elected if they are running in a parliamentary system with proportional representation, (b) an economic development approach that asserts that higher levels of economic development lead to higher levels of political participation and empowerment of all citizens, and (c) a cultural explanation that contends that women will not fare well politically if they come from a culture that devalues females and expects them to play traditional domestic roles.[13]

Kate has done a great job on her literature review in identifying possible key factors: institutions, economic development, and culture. If she concluded that economic development was the best predictor, she would generate the following model:

level of economic $\rightarrow$ level of electoral success
development   of females

Please notice that in formulating the model, Kate transformed the factors into "variables," things that can change. Thus, in the model section, she added the words "level of." While some models investigate correlations, this one asserts that causation flows in a particular direction. To find that the arrow is reversed would NOT substantiate this model, but compel the student to make a different argument.[14]

Looking at an example of a model from American politics, we could try to explain public attitudes toward the 2003 Iraq War and posit that ideology affects attitudes. Obviously, both attitudes and ideology can vary. People's opinions toward the war can range from strong support to strong opposition, with perhaps some even expressing no particular viewpoint, and in the U.S. context, there is a continuum

---

[13]Robert D. Putnam, *Making Democracy Work* (Princeton, NJ: Princeton University Press, 1993), pp. 9–12 and Pippa Norris and Ronald Inglehart, "Cultural Obstacles to Equal Representation," *Journal of Democracy* 12, no. 3 (2001): 126–140.

[14]Theodore J. Lowi made his career by reversing the causal arrow and claiming "policies cause politics" and not the other way around. That politics caused policy had been the conventional wisdom before Lowi came along. See his "American Business, Public Policy, Case Studies and Political Theory," *World Politics* 16 (1964): 677–715 and *The End of Liberalism: The Second Republic of the United States*, 2nd ed. (New York: W.W. Norton, 1979).

of ideologies, with the vast majority of the population placing themselves somewhere in between liberal and conservative. Thus, a researcher could posit the following model:

Extent of "liberal-ness" → attitudes toward 2003 Iraq War

The model implies that a person's view of the world affects how a person feels about a particular policy. The literature review that would have led to the creation of such a model would have explored the determinants of popular attitudes toward national (foreign) policies. The model, then, contends that ideology is the best explanation.

While the model is important for guiding your research, it is still incomplete. The model does not provide explicit information about the direction or the extent of the independent variable's effect on the dependent variable. From Kate's model, you don't know from the flow diagram what exactly will happen to female electoral success levels when economic development levels change. In fact, you may have no idea what the possible levels of economic development are. In the second example, a model accounting for support of the 2003 War, the impact of ideology is not explicitly identified. In both cases, you need something additional to communicate the *nature* of the relationship and the range of values the variables can take on—that is the **hypothesis.**

THE HYPOTHESIS

The best definition of the hypothesis is that it is your "best guess" about the links between the independent and dependent variables.[15] Of course, it is an educated guess, as you have surveyed the scholarly work on this question and assessed its logic in your literature review. Hypotheses[16] are often stated in the following terms:

1. for positive relationships: The more of X (the independent variable), the more of Y (the dependent variable)

2. for negative relationships: The more of X (the independent variable), the less of Y (the dependent variable)

---

[15]Janet Buttolph Johnson and Richard A. Joslyn, *Political Science Research Methods,* 3rd ed. (Washington, DC: Congressional Quarterly Press, 1995), pp. 53–54.

[16]This form applies to variables that take on continuous or interval values. The generic statement for hypotheses for data that are expressed as categories (nominal or ordinal data) will be discussed below.

So in Kate's model, the hypothesis that would follow would be:

> The greater the level of economic development in a state, the higher the percentage of females serving as elected officials in that country.

For the second example on ideology and attitudes, the hypothesis would be:

> the more liberal the person, the less likely the individual would support the war.

So the literature review defines the variables and helps you put forth a model; it will also tell you how the variables should relate to each other. You are not plucking these relationships from thin air, as you have uncovered them in your previous research. Still, explicitly writing this relationship out helps to keep you focused on your precise argument and, again, allows you to verify that your literature review accomplishes what it should. In Kate's case, the hypothesis reminds you that you are trying to determine whether increases in levels of economic development actually lead to increases in the levels of female elected officials. Note that in making this contention you are also saying the converse: decreases in development levels mean decreases in the numbers of women relative to men in public office. Similarly, with the second hypothesis, you are investigating whether ideological liberals are less likely to favor the Iraq war. Among more conservative people, you expect levels of support for the war to increase. In the first case, the variables are *positively* linked (higher levels of economic development lead to more women in parliament), and in the second, the relationship is *negative* (more liberal means less support).[17]

For both of our hypotheses, we can think of the values—levels of economic development, female elected officials, "liberal-ness," and support—as occurring on a continuum, and thus we call these **continuous** (also called **interval**) **variables.**[18] There are values for each that span a continuous spectrum and include all the gradations in between. But not all variables can be measured in this way; instead, some reflect *categories* in which we might be interested. For instance, we might wonder whether one type of institutional arrangement aids democratic consolidation better than another. The question is

---

[17]We could, however, generate a hypothesis with the *same* meaning, but that posits a direct relationship: "the more conservative an individual, the more likely he is to support the war."

[18]Please see Shively, pp. 61–62 for a discussion of continuous and discrete variables and the way these are linked to types of data—nominal, ordinal, and interval.

not simply academic, as constitution writers in states emerging from authoritarianism are likely to be searching for a system that will work. If those would-be authors read Juan J. Linz, then they are likely to be interested in the following hypothesis: parliamentary systems are more likely to lead to democratic consolidation than are presidential ones.[19] In this case, a governmental system is not more or less "parliamentary;" parliamentary and presidential systems do not fall on a continuum of some factor. Instead, a governmental system falls into the discrete category—parliamentary—or not; thus we call this a *discrete variable*.[20]

We have already seen some arguments that rely on discrete variables. In addition to Matt's argument about the Electoral College, the first two theses that I mentioned at the outset of the chapter—regarding the utility of the court and the ability of hard-liners to make peace—posit correlations between discrete (or category) variables. While researchers may not be sure nor care particularly *why* these occurrences happen, they are very interested in showing empirically that they have found an accurate description of reality. Thus, the contentions:

- In the United States, the Courts are not effective instruments of social change.

- Hard-liners are more likely to achieve peace with adversaries.

are hypotheses. But because the variables are not continuous, they cannot be accurately stated in the form "the more of X, the more (or less, if the relationship is negative) of Y." We still want to provide a hypothesis, however, to map out the precise direction of the relationships we expect to find. Thus, we can state as hypotheses "American Courts are less effective than legislatures as instruments of social change" and

---

[19]Juan J. Linz, "The Perils of Presidentialism," *Journal of Democracy* 1 no. 1 (1990): 51–69. Linz updated this article and replied to criticisms in a version published as the first chapter in Juan J. Linz and Arturo Valenzuela, eds., *The Limits of Presidential Democracy* (Baltimore: Johns Hopkins University Press, 1994). Please note that some have criticized Linz for not recognizing that there are at least three categories of governmental systems, the two mentioned and mixed or semi-presidential ones. See Anthony Mughan, review of *Presidentialism, Parliamentarism and Stable Democracy: The Failure of Presidential Democracy,* edited by Juan J. Linz and Arturo Valenzuela. *Mershon International Studies Review* 39 (1995): 123–125.

[20]Discrete variables can be ranked/ordinal (like "liberal-ness") or unranked/nominal (such as party affiliation) forms. In addition to continuous and discrete variables, mathematicians also identify dichotomous variables—variables that can take on only one of two variables, e.g. "yes/no," "on/off." In Social Science, we typically call these "dummy variables," that measure the presence or absence of a characteristic. For instance, we might be looking at Female/or not (i.e. male), Caucasian/or not, Catholic/or not.

"hard-liners are more likely than soft-liners to achieve peace with adversaries." Or as we saw in our example regarding governmental systems and democratic consolidation, "parliamentary systems are more likely than presidential ones to lead to the consolidation of democracy."

All papers, then, will make a contentious statement. If that argument is a causal or correlational one, the student should posit a model that isolates the variables (or key factors) and state a hypothesis that explains the nature of the relationship between them. While students writing normative and prescriptive papers need to advance a compelling thesis, they typically do not put forth a model.

APPLYING THESE INSIGHTS

As a result of your work in this chapter, you should be able to develop a thesis or a model and hypothesis section of your paper. The conclusion of your literature review should contain the kernel of your thesis, and with a little work for an empirical paper, it can be developed into a model and hypothesis. Why should this information already be in the conclusion of your literature review? Because in that section you put forth the best response to your research question. Thus, in asserting that a specific answer is preferred, you are making a contentious statement. Notice that you do not have to tell the reader explicitly "the thesis is . . . ." By concluding that one answer appears best and defending that choice you have effectively communicated that you have a thesis.

But what if you need to put forth a model and a hypothesis because you are investigating a correlation or causation? In that case, you have a little extra work to do and need an additional section—the Model and Hypothesis section—to express these ideas. As with the Literature Review Section, you should develop a specific title that fits your purposes and your paper. Here is how Diana, the third student we met in Chapter 2, handled this part of her paper in an early draft. Diana decided to investigate why the United States went to war with Iraq and not with North Korea in 2003.

CHAIN OF THOUGHT

Having delineated the various schools of thought about the influences on American foreign policy, constructivism seems to be the most useful approach for evaluating the differences in U.S. policies towards Iraq's and North Korea's

WMD programs. A causal chain can be used to outline the argument:

nature of American public perceptions of threats $\rightarrow$ type of U.S. foreign policy

The hypothesis for the constructivists is that the more American society has its eye fixed on a certain issue (that for a variety of factors it perceives a state or situation in a certain way), the more the United States will be prone to take serious action. Unlike realists who would argue that in the absence of a global sovereign, the United States engages in war to preserve itself and its interests, constructivists point to differences in the American public perceptions of the two states [Iraq and North Korea], arguing that the broader social understandings of the two countries played a major role in the differences in U.S. foreign policy.

With this section, Diana leaves no doubt in the minds of readers about what she is arguing.[21] And more importantly for her future work, she zeroed in on what she needs to investigate. She is going to look explicitly at public perceptions of threats and determine whether a view of more imminent dangers led to more aggressive U.S. responses, while a sense that a country was less hazardous provoked less hostile policies. In the Research Design section, Diana will define boundaries and defend the parameters she has set.

PRACTICAL SUMMARY

Before proceeding with the rest of the paper, you need to be able to state your argument precisely. That succinct formulation of your argument is the thesis; it is a "contentious statement" that can be upheld based on normative or logical principles or verified by data. If you are performing empirical research, your thesis will identify variables, and you will be interested in showing exactly why and how these factors are related. Thus, you will need a separate section in your paper that provides both your model (isolating the variables

---

[21]One criticism: she could have picked a title that told the reader about her argument. Do you have any suggestions?

that you will investigate and showing the direction in which causality operates) and your hypothesis (indicating the ways in which variables are related).

The steps I suggest that you follow when writing the Model and Hypothesis section are:

1. Return to the conclusion of your literature review and look carefully at which school of thought you believed was the most important. By choosing one approach, you are asserting a thesis. If you are working on empirical research, you would be well-served to create an additional section to state this argument in both its bare-bones (model) and relational (hypothesis) forms.

2. Identify the independent and dependent variables in your model. These variables should be apparent from the literature review. If they are not, you need to go back and rework your literature review so that it focuses on the factors that explain (possible independent variables) the development you are interested in studying (dependent variable).

3. Make sure, when putting forth the model, that the factors are stated in "variable" form. If you argued that "liberal-ness" best explains citizens' opinions on the 2003 war, you need to express the independent variable as the "extent of liberal-ness" when you transform this statement into a model. Then, separate the model from the rest of the text of the section so that it looks like the example from Diana's paper. If this is a causal relationship, there should be an arrow pointing from the independent to the dependent variable. (If you have more than one causal variable, include only one arrow and list the dependent variable only once. The independent variables are listed on the left, the arrow in the middle of the page, and the dependent variable on the right.)

4. Be sure that you know what kind of values (discrete or continuous) your variables will take on if you are performing empirical research.

5. Check that your hypothesis explains the ways in which changes in the independent variable affect the dependent variable. If you are using continuous data, your hypothesis can be stated in the following basic form: "The more of the independent variable, the more of the dependent variable," if the relationship is positive or "the more of the independent variable, the less of the dependent variable" for negative relations. Remember, category data will map into a different form of hypothesis that posits

particular outcomes for particular occurrences on the independent variable. For instance: "If social change is court-ordered, success will be lower than if social change is legislated."

6. Use a heading to separate the Model and Hypothesis section from the previous one. Try to pick a title that communicates what the section is about as well as what you are arguing. Remember, the section is short. It consists of
   a. A transitional sentence to link this discussion with the literature review.
   b. Some additional text to remind the reader of the thesis
   c. The actual model.
   d. Some text to explain the relationship that you expect between the independent and the dependent variables. (Here, you are also reminding the reader of what you learned in the literature review.)
   e. The actual hypothesis, stated in basic form.

SUGGESTED CALENDAR

If you're engaging in empirical research, I suggest that you complete a draft of both these first two sections at the same time because the Model and Hypothesis section follows so directly from the Literature Review. I recommend that these be finished by the end of the first third of your course, although your instructor may have a different timetable in mind. If you cannot identify a model and/or express a hypothesis, then you know that you have not properly done your literature review and you need some help. That's a great time to go see your professor or teaching assistant. When you do, bring your work so they can see exactly what you have been thinking and can help you more effectively and efficiently.

EXERCISES

1. Read the Op-Ed page in a recent *New York Times, Washington Post,* or *Wall Street Journal.* Identify the thesis of at least one of the authors. Can you also develop a corresponding hypothesis and model for that argument? Why or why not?

2. Read the front page of a recent *New York Times, Washington Post,* or *Wall Street Journal.* Develop at least one model and a

corresponding hypothesis from one of the articles that you read. What would you call the Model and Hypothesis section of a paper that explored the relationship you have identified?

3. Imagine that you wrote a literature review that contained these sentences in its conclusion:

> The "Money Talks" approach appears to be the best one for explaining why congressional representatives in competitive districts vote the way they do. Lobbyists and businesses who give enormous amounts of money receive access and sympathetic action on issues important to them from elected officials who are worried about staying in office. Constituent concerns, on the other hand, have less of an impact on these representatives when it is time to vote on legislation.

Develop a model and a hypothesis for this argument. What would you call the Model and Hypothesis section of this paper?

CHECKLIST FOR LITERATURE REVIEW (LR) & MODEL AND HYPOTHESIS (M&H)

Below is a checklist to consult while you are writing and before you turn in the first installment of your research paper, the Literature Review (LR) and Model and Hypothesis (M&H) sections. Any time you cannot check off an item, you need to go back and address the problem. Notice that I ask you not only to master methodological issues but to improve your writing skills. We each have certain strengths and weaknesses as writers, and you will only get better if you pay close attention to the issues that give you difficulty. For instance, your professor should not have to tell you repeatedly to avoid passive voice. If that's one of your tendencies, look for passive voice in your text and change these constructions before handing in your paper.

1. Does your paper have a cover page consistent with the format style your professor has selected?   _____

2. Does each section of your paper have an appropriate, descriptive title?   _____

3. Does the LR have an introductory paragraph that introduces the reader to the purpose of the section?   _____

4. Does the M&H section begin with at least one transitional sentence linking it with the work that you did in the LR? _____

5. Have you clearly stated your research question in your Literature Review, but not in question form? _____

6. Have you provided different scholarly answers to that question and grouped these answers into schools of thought, each with its own label? Have you named the adherents to the school and explained its logic as fairly as possible? _____

7. Have you explained the weaknesses and strengths of the different schools? _____

8. Have you written a concluding paragraph for your literature review that explains which school you prefer and why? _____

9. If you are writing an empirical paper, is the model stated in a flow diagram, similar to the student example? _____

10. If you are writing an empirical paper, are the elements of the model clearly variables (i.e. things that can take on different values and change)? _____

11. If you are writing an empirical paper, is the hypothesis explicitly stated and is it in the proper form ("the more of X, the more/less of Y"— depending on whether the relationship is positive or negative—OR "If X is A, then Y is B, but if X is C, then Y is D")? _____

12. Have you properly cited the sources of your ideas and kept direct quotes to a minimum? Have you avoided plagiarism? (You should have *at least* one citation per paragraph in the literature review, with the exception perhaps of the introductory and concluding paragraphs. And note that you can cite more than one source in a footnote, OR you can cite several pages of the same source in one footnote). Do all these citations appear in the form your professor has specified? _____

13. If you have used a long quote, have you indented it and NOT included quotation marks, unless you have a quote

within a quote? (See a style manual on how to handle long quotes.) _____

14. Have you MINIMIZED your use of long quotes? _____

15. Have you run the spell and grammar check, but recognized that it is imperfect? _____

16. Have you numbered your pages? _____

17. Did you include a bibliography that conforms to the style format your professor chose? _____

18. Recognizing the limits of spell and grammar check, have you edited your paper? _____

19. Add your own personal writing concerns (check relevant ones):
    - split infinitives _____
    - sentence fragments _____
    - run-on sentences _____
    - good transitions _____
    - word choice/overuse of words _____
    - homonym confusion _____
    - overuse of pronouns _____
    - passive voice _____
    - appropriate length of paragraphs (more than one sentence, less than a page) _____
    - other _____ _____
    - other _____ _____

5

Enticing the Reader and Drawing a Road Map: Writing an Introduction and Developing a Title

Y ou may be surprised to hear this, but after writing your Literature Review and developing your thesis, you are ready to write your Introduction and think of a title for your paper. Once you've come up with a good research question, writing a strong Introduction and developing an appropriate title are your most important tasks because these items make a first impression on the reader. As you've probably been told, first impressions are very important! The title prepares the reader for the contents in brief, and the Introduction provides an overview of your paper. Your Introduction also serves as a type of contract between you and the reader, establishing the parameters of your work. The contract is, however, double-edged. Whatever you promise in the Introduction, you must deliver, but a reader cannot expect you to do more than you have reasoned is necessary (as long as your logic is sound). Be very sure that in the rest of your paper you address all of the points that you make in the Introduction or the reader will be able to identify weaknesses in your essay by pointing to your own words and demonstrating that you did not uphold your promises.

ELEMENTS OF A GOOD INTRODUCTION

Very basically and obviously, an Introduction introduces the reader to your research paper. It does so by communicating the puzzle you are investigating, usually not in question form[1]—why that puzzle is interesting and important to a general reader as well as to a specialist audience (social scientists, policy professionals, and elected officials)—and providing a "road map" to the rest of the paper. Looking at the three elements of this description, you should feel heartened because if you have followed the process recommended in Chapter 2 for developing your research question, you already have written a paragraph that accomplishes two of these elements. You may simply want to rework your notes to better entice the reader and immediately present the interesting and important puzzle you are trying to solve. Your "sell" of the paper should not be too long, as you neither want to bore the reader nor provide details that would be better left to later sections. In fact, you can probably satisfy these first two elements in three to five sentences.

The third part of the Introduction—providing the road map—is more difficult. You have probably never written a research paper, so the general form is new to you, and you haven't performed your research yet, so you are not quite sure what you will find. But you have worked hard to develop the conceptual framework of the paper; you understand the schools of thought, and in many cases, the models that follow from them; you have even developed a hypothesis or thesis. So, even with the indecision and dearth of research, you should still take a stab at writing the Introduction, including the road map. This is a *draft,* and getting your ideas and overall plan down on paper will help you enormously in writing each subsequent section and performing your research and analysis.

Before we go further, let me better explain the "road map" concept. I am talking about a basic sketch or outline of your whole paper.

---

[1]You can often find excellent works of research that state a well-crafted research question as the first (or an early) sentence of the paper. If you are having trouble getting started, certainly consider using your question as a jumping-off point.

If you drew a map to help someone get somewhere, it would be incomplete but hit the major landmarks: Route I95N to exit 40, south on Rt. 129 for .6 miles, left on Cherry Lane, to the fourth house on the right. A map corresponding to these directions does not fill in other details about the highway or show the lake you know is off Route 129. It provides the specifics someone needs to get to the destination: no more and no less. The goal for your Introduction is to do the same. To achieve this, you need to know what each part of the upcoming paper is supposed to accomplish in theory and have some general idea of what, in particular, you will be doing in those sections. Let's review the sections of the paper.

Section 1: Introduction
Section 2: Literature Review
Section 3: Model and Hypothesis
Section 4: Research Design
Section 5: Analysis and Assessment
Section 6: Conclusion

As you already know from Chapter 3, the Literature Review surveys the scholarly answers to your research question and identifies the major schools of thought. If necessary, the model isolates the causal variables underlying your preferred approach, and the hypothesis is your "best guess" response to your research question. As we saw in Chapter 1 (and will learn more about subsequently), the Research Design is the plan for actually performing your work, whereas the Analysis and Assessment Section examines information in order to evaluate your hypothesis. Lastly, the Conclusion allows you to reflect on what you found and consider directions for new research.

In the final draft, your Introduction will contain one or perhaps two sentences for each of the sections of your paper. In the early drafts, however, you will do well to mention the schools of thought and to focus on one of them as the one that you think is best. In addition, you should strive to identify your case or cases (what specific instances of the general phenomenon you are going to study) and make another guess about what you will find.

Since this book is written with the assumption that you will be writing each section as you are proceeding through this text, I will spend time here explaining how to write a *first draft* of the Introduction. I will return to the Introduction in the last chapter to remind you to be sure that your final draft of this section accomplishes all that it needs—entices the reader and provides an accurate and up-to-date road map of your paper.

You may still feel that you are not ready to write your Introduction, and some other writing guides would agree. They counsel to write this section last.[2] I contend, however, that you've done sufficient work to write a *draft* of the Introduction now. In fact, putting your ideas on paper will be an excellent exercise in clear thinking at this point, because in the Introduction, you must be able to communicate succinctly each piece of your paper. Working on the Introduction will help you sharpen your Literature Review and model and hypothesis or thesis, while requiring you to think about the cases, the ways you will study this problem, and the information you need to gather. In essence, writing your Introduction propels you forward at this stage. I have seen many students become bogged down in the research for the theoretical framework for a paper (Literature Review, model and thesis/hypothesis) and not make progress on the next phases. The scholarly literature is difficult, and the temptation to read more and tinker continuously with your understanding of the perspectives and any corresponding models and hypotheses leads to inertia. To prevent you from getting stuck in this swamp of theory and articulation, you need to make your research plan explicit and start thinking about your findings earlier rather than later. At this point, you don't need to be "*right,*" you just need to be on the "*right track.*"

Thus, as you work on your first draft of the Introduction, you should feel prepared as well as a little daring. You have the information to express what your research question is, why it is interesting, and why it is important. You even have an understanding of the different schools of thought and have made a decision about which one you favor. Now you have to make a guess about what cases you will study, how you will investigate them, and what you will find. Again, this is not easy, but it is *possible* at this stage of the process. Be bold! What do you *think* you will find? As you make your guesses, remember that if after you finish your work, you don't find what you expected at the beginning, there's no harm done. You can always change your Introduction by adding some text to explain that you could not confirm your hypothesis, for instance. The point is to *learn through this process* and to "get it right" at the end.

---

[2] See, for example, Eviatar Zerubavel, *The Clockwork Muse: A Practical Guide to Writing Theses, Dissertations, and Books* (Cambridge, MA: Harvard University Press, 1999), p. 54.

CAN YOU REALLY WRITE AN
INTRODUCTION NOW? ONE EXAMPLE

You are now ready to write a first draft of your Introduction. You have a basic outline of your paper at this point, although admittedly, the last three sections are rather thin. Your outline and your Introduction are very closely linked. Both are road maps for the paper, but with different audiences: The Introduction is for external readers and the outline is for you. What would your outline look like at this point? Each section of your paper corresponds to a Roman numeral in your outline, and you have begun to fill in these sections so that you have something to write up. For instance,

I. Introduction
    A. Research Question as a puzzle
    B. Why interesting and important?
    C. Road Map
II. Literature Review
    A. Schools of thought
    B. Why is one school better than the others?
III. Model and Hypothesis
    A. Model: What are the independent and dependent variables?
    B. Hypothesis: How are these variables related to one another?

Although you have little done work on the later sections, you know from the first chapter that they will look something like this (with more parts to be filled in later):

IV. Research Design
    A. Exactly how will I know the values of my variables?
    B. Exactly what cases will I study and why?
V. Analysis and Assessment
    A. How will my hypothesis guide me through my cases?
    B. If my hypothesis holds, what will I find in these cases?
VI. Conclusion
    A. What will my findings mean for theory, policy, and general civic concerns?

Start with the first two points of Roman numeral I and then, under "Road Map," include summaries of the rest of the outline (II–VI), writing one or two sentences for each section of the paper. A wise strategy might be to consult the end of the first chapter of this book to remind yourself of the basic goals of these later sections as you're working on your introduction.

You might think I am still asking for the impossible. But look at the example of Diana, the student who was really interested in understanding anti-proliferation policy and the Iraq War. Here is her early attempt at writing the Introduction to a paper examining why in 2003 the United States intervened militarily in Iraq, but did not take up arms against North Korea:

> The morning of September 11th was one of the most catastrophic in the history of the United States, a day which created a mentality of fear across the country. The Bush Administration was faced with the monumental tasks of answering the problems of global terrorism, anti-American sentiment, and having to deal with rogue states. In the wake of the attacks, the United States' national interests have been increasingly driven by the desire and need for national security. The international community has long pointed to specific rogue states and the dangers they pose, primarily regarding weapons of mass destruction (WMD). In his "Axis of Evil" speech, President Bush focused on Iraq and North Korea as two of the states presenting the most imminent threats to the United States. Each state was dealt with differently; North Korea diplomatically, while Iraq was met with war. Theories of international politics can be utilized to explain this discrepancy in policy. Institutionalist liberals contend that the domestic electoral institutions of the United States play a role. Proponents of the realist school of thought point to the anarchic nature of the international system and the balance of power which exists between states. Lastly, the constructivists offer the strongest argument, stating that the national interests and policies of the United States are socially constructed.[3]

> Constructivism best explains the discrepancy in American policies towards Iraq and North Korea. Both are similar cases, having WMD and/or the will to produce them, and both were un-democratic states posing a threat to United States' security. The difference between the two can be best explained by the

---

[3]For the institutionalist, neo-realist, and constructivist perspectives, see Miroslav Nincic, "U.S. Soviet Policy and the Electoral Connection," *World Politics* 42 (1990): 370–96, Kenneth Waltz, "Origins of War in Neorealist Theory," *Journal of Interdisciplinary History* 18, no. 4 (1988): 39–52, Alexander Wendt, "Constructing International Politics," *International Security* 20, no. 1 (Summer 1995): 71–81.

constructivist theory, showing how the interests of a state come from the societal consensus on the issues at hand. The constructivist paradigm can be used to explain how in the wake of September 11th, the American frame of mind was more hostile towards the Middle Eastern region as a whole, thus explaining aggression towards Iraq and diplomatic negotiations with North Korea.

You'll note that Diana starts out by introducing the historical context in which this intervention occurred as a way of justifying why her research question is interesting and important. Second, she clearly states the different intellectual approaches to answering her question, the cases that she will examine, and why they are comparable. In concluding this section, she asserts her preferred perspective. Great job, particularly at this early stage of the game. In later drafts, Diana will want to include more about the last sections of her paper. She hasn't really indicated how she will do her data analysis or exactly what pieces of evidence make her confident that her argument holds. Lastly, she would do well to flesh out more clearly what her research suggests about other, similar cases and to consider the political and policy implications of her findings.

The bottom line: Diana's first attempt at an Introduction is strong. She entices the reader by identifying a compelling puzzle, and she provides about one sentence to summarize each section of the following essay. Yes, Diana needs to find a way to discuss the Analysis and Assessment and Conclusion, but remember, this is only the first draft!

ANOTHER ELEMENT IN ATTRACTING READERS: DEVELOPING AN APPEALING TITLE

Diana has one more task to complete before she submits this draft of her work to her professor. She needs to come up with a title for her paper. A title should do three things: communicate your question or puzzle, identify your cases or the specifics of your study, and summarize your argument or thesis. Yet you have a limited number of words—if the Introduction is the paper in brief, the title is the microscopic view. Because you're trying to accomplish so much in so few words, you'll often need to use a colon to separate the ideas. While such a title is often not the most "literary" or clever, it is consistent with our notion of a first impression and the contract: Readers will be very clear about your topic and your argument. They will know what to expect and what you are promising to deliver. Again, you may not feel ready to put a name on your research project. Remember that this is a working draft title and that you are likely to modify it as you continue writing.

Considering where you are in the research process, you're in a better position to communicate what your puzzle is than to identify your cases or state your findings. You'll have to rely on your best guesses and assume that your title, just as all the other parts of the paper, will develop over time. You will impress your reader, however, if at this early stage you can come up with a title that accomplishes as many of these goals as possible. By stating the puzzle and findings in such a short form (a phrase for each), you are forcing yourself to formulate as precisely as possible what you are studying and arguing.

Given my recommendations—state the puzzle, the cases, and the (expected) findings—what should Diana call her paper? One possibility is "Understanding the Bush Administration's Anti-Proliferation Policy: A Constructivist Approach." Another is "To Intervene or Not to Intervene: The Social Construction of 21st Century American Anti-Proliferation Policy." Both of these communicate the topic, the cases, and the argument. Thus they are great working drafts. I would guess that you could come up with other titles, too. There is no "right" one, but you need to learn to distinguish between one that doesn't serve you well—fails to communicate the question, cases, and argument—and one that does.

Once you have the basics for the name, see if you can make it more appealing. You can greatly help your effort to attract readers if you can develop a "catchy" title, although coming up with one that doesn't sound silly can be difficult. Be *very careful* that your imaginative title is appropriate for a formal writing assignment and that its meaning will be obvious to the reader. Recently, I read a paper with a title that quoted a famous Rolling Stones' song lyric: "'You Can't Always Get What You Want, But If You Try, You Get What You Need': The Confirmation Process of Justices of the Supreme Court."[4] The wittiness of this title was initially lost on both me and a colleague. The author never made clear the relationship of the song title to her argument (that in recent years the Senate

---

[4]Michelle Castle, "'You Can't Always Get What You Want, But If You Try, You Get What You Need': The Confirmation Process of Justices of the Supreme Court." (Senior Honors Thesis, Saint Joseph's University, 2005).

Judiciary Committee has used the code word "privacy" as a proxy for assessing a nominee's position on abortion). My colleague was a fan of only classical music, so he had no idea of the allusion. To make this quote work, the author should have explained the connection between the Stones and her argument in at least her Introduction and Conclusion. Moreover, the song passage was too long. The writer could simply have said, "'You Can't Always Get What You Want': The Confirmation Process of Justices of the Supreme Court," because if the author explains the allusion, the reader will understand her point with the short form of the song title.

Some of the authors that we've already encountered in this book have been very successful with their titles. Consider

- Theodore J. Lowi, *The End of Liberalism: The Second Republic of the United States,* 2nd ed. (New York: W.W. Norton, 1979)

- John J. Mearsheimer, "Back to the Future: Instability in Europe after the Cold War," *International Security* 15 (1990), 5–56

- Robert D. Putnam, *Bowling Alone: The Collapse and Revival of American Community* (New York: Simon & Schuster, 2000)

- Gerald Rosenberg, *The Hollow Hope: Can Courts Bring About Social Change?* (Chicago: University of Chicago Press, 1991)

- Alexander Wendt, "Anarchy Is What States Make of It: The Social Construction of Power Politics," *International Organization* 46 (1992): 391–425

For all of these titles, the short form (up to the colon) is *surprising, provocative, evocative, alliterative,* and/or *suggestive of another famous work.* Thus, the title is likely to jump out at a reader. In addition, both the first and second parts of all these titles communicate important information about the subject and argument. Thus, these are all great titles. Of course, because their content was so compelling, these works became must-reads. As we continue with our discussion on Research Design, you will learn how to continue to develop your plan to make your paper notable, too.

PRACTICAL SUMMARY

The Introduction and title of your paper are very important because they make a first impression on your reader. Your goal is to make a positive one, attracting readers to your work. In addition, the

Introduction and title are like a contract with the reader; in them, you state what you will accomplish in your paper, and you need to deliver on those promises. The Introduction and title are closely related, with the Introduction as your paper in brief and your title as the miniaturized version. When you write your Introduction, you should seek to accomplish three tasks, in the following order:

1. Communicate your research question as a puzzle.
2. Explain why this question is interesting and important.
3. Provide a road map to your paper.

The first two tasks convince the reader to read the paper, the road map—based on the outline of the paper—sets out your course so the reader knows what to expect on this read/ride. The major sections of the outline correspond with the separate parts of the research paper, some of which you have already written. Your goal in the Introduction is to write a sentence or sometimes two, summarizing each section.[5]

Your title seeks to convey, in as memorable phrasing as possible,

1. the puzzle
2. the cases
3. the argument

Typically, your title will have two parts to it, separated by a colon. At this stage in the research process, both your Introduction and title are preliminary, as you will want to return to them later to be sure that your findings are what you predicted. Still, you're off to a great start, and you will be glad that you have put these ideas on paper as you begin work on the Research Design.

SUGGESTED CALENDAR

About a third of the way through the research process, you should begin working on the draft of your Introduction and your title. You will feel unready to write both, but you can do it. You have done enough work to put your ideas on paper, and the exercise of writing will help clarify your ideas and propel you forward into the later stages of the research process.

---

[5] I am assuming that your paper is in the 10–20 page range. For longer papers, you will likely need a longer Introduction because you will write more to preview each part of a more extensive work.

EXERCISES

1. Look at the following first paragraph to an almost 500-page book. What do you see the authors, Steven L. Burg and Paul S. Shoup, accomplishing here that you will also be doing in your Introduction? What else must they do in the rest of this section to complete an effective Introduction?

> In this volume, we examine the dynamics of ethnic conflict in Bosnia-Herzegovina, and the dilemmas surrounding international involvement in it. We analyze the causes and conduct of the war; why, for more than three years, international efforts to resolve the conflict in Bosnia failed; and why they finally succeeded in late 1995. We review the Dayton accord produced in 1995 and ask whether, after two years of experience with its implementation, we can expect it to lead to long-term peace in Bosnia. Our analyses are intended to help citizens interested in understanding and learning from the events in Bosnia-Herzegovina; scholars attempting to understand the dynamic of ethnic conflict and develop strategies for managing it; and policymakers intent on preventing ethnic conflicts from undermining international peace.[6]

2. Write an outline for Diana's Introduction. Can you think of two more possible titles for that research paper?

3. Imagine that Tom, the student who wanted to write about sports arenas and economic development, has written the following outline for his paper. Write an Introduction and develop a title that corresponds with Tom's outline.

   I. Paying for sports stadiums—When does it benefit cities?
      A. Interesting and important because many cities want to be the home to major and minor league teams. Teams often demand subsidies for their arenas. When and to what extent should cities (and their citizens) pay? Urban areas often face very tight budgets and many priorities, while sports owners and players are frequently multi-millionaires.
      B. Topic continues to be relevant as several cities have recently faced, or are faced with, this question.

---

[6]Steven L. Burg and Paul S. Shoup, *The War in Bosnia-Herzegovina: Ethnic Conflict and International Intervention* (Armonk, NY: ME Sharpe, 1999), p. 3.

    C. Question is actually a puzzle: Should cities pay so that athletes will continue to play, when those same municipalities can't afford to fund many necessities—e.g., public transit and education—adequately?

II. Three schools of thought[7]
    A. Nay-sayers: Public funds should not be used for what is primarily private (the team owner's) gain.
    B. Yes-men: Having a sports team (especially a major league one) is good for the city's image and morale. Losing a team puts the city in the ranks of "lesser places," disappoints fans, hurts surrounding businesses, and may convince other economic actors to leave, too. Even if the team isn't threatening to leave, a better stadium will attract more attendance and increase spending in and around the arena. Thus, cities generally should find the money when owners come asking.
    C. Qualified Optimists: If stadiums are frequently used, integrated into a neighborhood (i.e., close to other attractions), and aesthetically pleasing, then public funds might be used well here. Under these conditions, the stadium spurs further investment and improvement in the neighborhood and throughout the city.

III. Preferred Approach: Qualified Optimists—providing money for any development project does not always create widespread benefits. Public money needs to be used very carefully. Stadiums bring about positive economic benefits when they are: used frequently, integrated into an appropriate city neighborhood, and attractive.

IV. Research Design
    A. Why these Cases: Baltimore's Camden Yards vs. New England's Gillette Stadium. Maximize variance on the three key factors.
        1. Baseball plays over 80 games per year at their home field (Camden Yards) versus football which plays fewer than 10 (Gillette). Note, however, that fields are sometimes used for other purposes (e.g., concerts).

---

[7] I am not providing citations here because I do not want to do the vast majority of the work for someone's research paper. If this topic is interesting to you, pursue it. It won't take you long to find the debate and to reconsider whether I have actually identified the proper variables and made the "best" argument.

2. Baltimore's park is integrated into the city, near another attraction—the Inner Harbor—and not far from downtown, while New England's is situated in the suburbs, convenient to Providence, Boston, and a major highway, but not near any other interesting destinations.

3. Aesthetics were very important (not only in terms of properly situating it in the neighborhood but in the design of the ballpark itself) in Baltimore and not in Foxboro.

B. Independent Variables: level of usage, level of integration, attractiveness.

C. Dependent Variables: level of benefit of stadium (note: economic and cultural/prestige components). Measured by amount of other private investment in the area, taxes and funds generated from this region since the stadium opened, perception of this city/area as a "place to be." (Need to scale by the level of public money city spent, i.e., benefits gained per dollar spent.)

D. Data Sources: local newspapers, city/regional development offices, interviews with local officials.

V. Assessment

A. Baltimore's park is a big success, has helped revitalize Baltimore. City and team did everything "right" in this case. Cities in New England (and their states) made a big mistake by not trying to lure the stadium home and not doing it "right."

VI. A study of Camden Yards and Gillette Stadium upholds the view of the Qualified Optimists. Under certain conditions, public money is well-spent in aiding the construction of sports stadiums in cities, but these conditions are very specific. The stadium must be used frequently, well-integrated into the city and close to other urban attractions, and aesthetically pleasing.

6

Making Your Plan and Protecting Yourself from Criticism: The Research Design

With the conceptual framework of your paper completed, you have one more step to undertake before proceeding with your analysis: the Research Design. By now you're at mile 13 in the marathon. You're halfway done, but you're starting to hurt. How are you going to make it? This is a difficult point, but if you can just keep going the excitement and adrenaline rush that will come from being ever-closer to the end will propel you on. Just hang in there and keep working.

The Research Design is where you plan exactly what you will do to determine whether your thesis is sustained or not.[1] It is also the

---

[1]For detailed and methodologically sensitive discussions of research design see Donald T. Campbell and Julian C. Stanley, *Experimental and Quasi-Experimental Designs for Research* (Boston: Houghton Mifflin, 1963), W. Phillips Shively, *The Craft of Political Research,* 5th ed. (Upper Saddle River, NJ: Prentice Hall, 2002), pp. 72–94, and W. Laurence Neuman, *Social Research Methods: Qualitative and Quantitative Methods,* 5th ed. (Boston: Allyn & Bacon, 2003), pp. 137–168.

section in your paper where you explicitly defend the choices you make regarding how to translate your concepts into "know-able" entities, what instances of the phenomenon you are going to study, and what sources or information you will use to perform this research. In effect, the Research Design is a first line of defense against criticism on your "follow through" in the project: you present the logic for your decisions so that readers can see that you have made the best choices about how to proceed, given the limitations that face social scientists (i.e., not rocket scientists!)[2] regarding concept formation and translation, case selection, data availability, and general design issues.

Typically, the Research Design section completes three and sometimes four tasks:

1. The definition of concepts and the establishment of a strategy for measuring them
2. The selection of cases for study
3. The identification of sources of information for your analysis
4. The writing of instruments (such as surveys or interview questionnaires) for generating information

Typically, you must defend your choices here as the "best" for evaluating your thesis given the time and other resource constraints under which you are operating.

CONCEPT DELINEATION
AND MEASUREMENT

By the time you reach the Research Design, you have identified a research question, written your introduction, reviewed the literature, and developed a thesis or a model and hypothesis. The next step is to determine how you are going to evaluate your argument. Your first task is to translate your concepts (what we earlier called variables) into identifiable entities. In Chapter 4, we looked at several

---

[2]Shively, p. 17.

"contentious statements" for which the nature of the relationship between the concepts was not of central importance to the author. These included

- Hobbes is an opponent of liberal associationalism; he defends and supports royal rule. He is, therefore, not a forefather of liberalism as some have contended.[3]

- Religion was (and should continue to be) central to the formation of the American government and governance. The American identity is (and should continue to be) Protestant.[4]

Even with these types of theses, however, paper writers need to think about how they are going to define and "measure" their concepts. Each of these statements contains notions that must be carefully delineated

- "opponent of liberal associationalism," "defender and supporter of royal rule," "liberalism"

- "religion," "central to American government and governance," "American identity," "Protestant identity"

For absolute clarity, a researcher needs to explain precisely what each of these terms means, both in the abstract and for the actual research.[5] Taking the first example, then, an analyst needs to explain what "liberal associationalism" and "liberalism" mean and how she is going to know when Hobbes is arguing for or against them. In the research design, the writer thus establishes standards that guide her through her project: they help her be sure that what she is finding is what she "knows" and not simply what she "wants to know" or what she "thinks." In other words, by setting out clear definitions and steps for evaluating her concepts, a researcher develops a transparent system for determining her assessments. She does not measure or evaluate yet; she simply states her plan in this portion of the paper. Again, following this example, the writer would provide her definitions (for liberal associationalism, royal rule, and

---

[3]Richard Boyd, "Thomas Hobbes and the Perils of Pluralism," *The Journal of Politics* 63 (2001), 392–413.

[4]Samuel P. Huntington, *Who Are We? The Challenges to America's National Identity* (New York: Simon & Schuster, 2004).

[5]In addition, one's analysis is generally more credible if methods are spelled out specifically and therefore can be replicated by another investigator.

liberalism) and the key words or phrases that she will use to note Hobbes' opposition to the first, and defense and support of the second. Moreover, her definition of liberalism will be linked to positions on these key concepts (liberal associationalism and absolutist rule), and therefore, Hobbes' stance on the first two points will affect his ability to be a source of liberal thought. This is her *plan* for determining the extent to which Hobbes is an opponent of active social groups, a defender of royal rule, and therefore an opponent of liberal ideas. The writer will be well-served to explain this final logical connection in her research design, too, stating for instance "because of liberalism's belief that a vibrant civil society benefits the life of the polity as a whole and its firm commitment to the equality of all individuals, someone who is opposed to the role and fluidity of groups in society and supports the hierarchy of monarchical rule cannot be a forefather of liberalism." By making an explicit plan and clearly laying out her logic, the writer works to eliminate wishful thinking or other flaws when she actually performs the analysis at a later point in time.

Empirical researchers also have to use great care with concept definition and the translation of concepts into actual variables. When we set out our models in Chapter 4 we were technically identifying the key concepts that we believed were related to each other. To make them true variables, we **operationalize** the concepts by transforming the theoretical ideas into actual measures. Where does any researcher—whether assessing a thesis or a model—find guides to specifying and measuring concepts? One of the best sources is other authors who have investigated similar questions or concepts. It is perfectly acceptable to use their definitions and measurement strategies as long as you give the authors credit! Where will you find these ideas? Go back to the authors you identified in your literature review and look at how they arrived at their answers—what choices did they make when conceiving of their variables? What kind of methods did they employ to measure them? Pick from among the approaches and explicitly defend all of the choices that you make by explaining them in your text.

There is often a problem, however, with using existing work as your sole guide to specifying and operationalizing your concepts: Established scholars may have access to far more resources (e.g., time, money, research assistance, information) than you do. One of my favorite examples to use for teaching students about research and research paper writing is Robert Putnam's *Making Democracy Work*.[6] Putnam's study, however, took about two decades, involved many research assistants, and required a number of large grants to complete. Thus, he was able to develop measures for variables that used multiple indicators, required the interviews of legions of local officials, and consisted of many statistical sources. If you were interested in probing the importance of culture versus economic development in explaining the efficacy of democracy in different regions of the United States, you might take Putnam's work as an inspiration, but you certainly could not strictly apply his approaches to measuring variables.[7] You would have to modify the strategies to make them "doable," yet still logically sustainable.

Sometimes, if you have consulted purely theoretical articles in your Literature Review to help you answer your general question, you will be able write an excellent section on the theoretical debate, but these articles will be a poor guide at the Research Design stage. In this case, you need to find additional studies, ones that are more applied, dealing with real-world cases, and seek to assess an argument similar to your own. Compare the way concepts are defined and measured and pick one out of the new set that you find "best." Or, if you feel confident that translating the concepts into knowable entities is relatively straightforward, you can advance a plan based on your own logic.

Let's look at an example of operationalizing concepts for an empirical paper to understand this process better. Suppose we were interested in investigating the hypothesis, "the greater the imbalance of power between two states, the greater the probability of war." The corresponding model would be

$$\text{the nature of the balance of power} \rightarrow P(\text{war})$$

How are we going to know what the level of the balance or the probability of war is? These concepts cannot be immediately found as

---

[6]Other works that provide great examples of measurement strategies include Manus Midlarsky, ed., *Handbook of War Studies II* (Ann Arbor: University of Michigan Press, 2000) and John A. Vasquez and Marie T. Henehan, *The Scientific Study of Peace and War: A Text Reader* (Lanham, MD: Lexington Books, 1999).

[7]Robert D. Putnam, with Robert Leonardi and Raffaella Y. Nanetti, *Making Democracy Work: Civic Traditions in Modern Italy* (Princeton, NJ: Princeton University Press, 1993).

values in some source. Here is where we must make some choices. Let's start by trying to understand the balance of power. There is no place where we can simply look up that figure, so we have some work to do. The first step is to find the power position of each state, but that value is not listed anywhere either. Well, we will have to make decisions and provide justifications to determine it. Suppose we think that the amount of money a state spends on defense, the number of people in its military, and the number of weapons of mass destruction that it possesses all contribute to power position. We have to explain why we think these are the best **indicators** of national power. Good justifications might be that these are what experts contend are most important or that these factors have had the most impact on past conflicts between these states or on other similar, recent conflicts. Having determined the components of national power, we must now come up with an assessment of the *balance of power*. The notion of the "balance" suggests the extent to which the force levels are approximately equal or out of line. How can we capture this idea? One way would be to come up with an equation to weight the importance of these three factors (spending, people, WMD) and look at the ratio of State A's to State B's holdings to arrive at the balance. The closer the ratio is to "1," the closer the forces are to being balanced. But the ratio could range from a very small fraction (if B were far stronger) to a very large number (if A were far stronger). If we were to advance a formula, we would have a quantitative representation of the military balance. Note that we would have to explain why we were establishing the weights that we choose. For instance, one example could be

$$\text{Balance} = \frac{0.3 \times \text{mil spending in A} + 0.5 \times \text{force size of A} + 0.2 \times \text{A's WMD holdings}}{0.3 \times \text{mil spending in B} + 0.5 \times \text{force size of B} + 0.2 \times \text{B's WMD holdings}}$$

The best way to come up with a formula would be to find a scholar who has tried to quantify the value of the balance. Lacking that, we could provide on our own weights and logic. We might argue that the terrain of the area made person power most important and in previous conflicts State A had not used its WMD, so force size was weighted more heavily than WMD. Moreover, we could also contend that military spending reflected the quality of the armed forces, and we wanted to capture the different capabilities of the militaries in this situation. No matter which approach we follow, we should take care to recognize that *our number is not some actual balance, but our attempt to determine the value.*

We could take another approach to estimating the balance between these two states, by providing a qualitative assessment. This means that we will not arrive at a number for the value (in the same way that we did not use numbers when trying to evaluate the hypothesis on Hobbes). In the case of the military balance, we consider the impact of the three indicators and the way the totals compare to each other qualitatively, too. In doing that, we state in words our sense of the weighting: force size is most important, followed by military spending and nuclear holdings.

As you can plainly see, regardless of which approach (numeric or word representation of the values) we choose, we have begun to make some important decisions for our variables. These can have a huge impact on the study. Because we have to translate our concepts into variables we have to be very careful that our measures are both *valid* and *reliable*. In other words, we want our variables to be valid, that is, accurate representations of our concepts (or at least as accurate as possible). If we think of operationalizing as a game of darts, then we achieve validity when our measures hit the target of the concept on the bull's eye. But we can't be accurate only sometimes; we don't want to be a wild hurler who can hit the bull's eye on one throw and land a dart in another patron's pizza on the next one. That's where reliability enters the discussion. Reliable measures are ones that you or anyone else can employ at any time and arrive at the same assessment of the variable. So, a measure is reliable when it repeatedly hits the same small area on the dart board. A measure that is both valid and reliable consistently hits the bull's eye. A measure that is valid but unreliable will scatter around the bull's eye unpredictably, while a measure that is reliable but invalid will always land in the same vicinity but never hit the center. Using darts as an analogy, you can see that having a valid and reliable measure is important.

In the Research Design section, you need to have an explicit discussion of why your measures are as valid and reliable as possible. Please note that in this example you might have to explain and defend yourself in numerous ways. First, you need to defend your choice of indicators for your notion of state power. This discussion, of course, directly relates to the validity of your measure. You might have excluded defense spending, so why did you choose to include it? Is it really necessary? Why? Here is where you can explain that you are using the indicators that scholars have used or that these three make sense for a certain set of reasons. Whatever your logic, include it so that your reader can follow your reasoning. Second, you need to defend your weighting scheme to the reader, whether you are providing a quantitative or qualitative assessment of the balance. Again, having scholarly backing for your decision is an excellent defense, but you can also provide your own compelling reasoning. Third, you must protect yourself against charges that your method or your conduct during the assessment will introduce bias and therefore make the measures unreliable. When you are simply reading numbers off an existing table from another data source, it is hard for you to introduce bias unless you mistakenly read the wrong column or row. Thus, as long as you use care, the step of gathering the data with which to determine the strength of each side should be reliable. But is the calculation of the balance also highly reliable? When you provide a mathematical formula, no matter what mood you are (or anyone else is) in, you will get the same values for any incident of your variable as long as you read the tables properly and don't make a silly arithmetic mistake. Thus, the quantitative approach is very transparent and can be repeated by others wanting to replicate your study. It is highly reliable. Quantification for something like the military balance (which some might argue is highly subjective), however, might give the researcher a false sense of accuracy. "I can calculate a number; therefore that number must have real meaning, right?" Beware of **reifying** these values, coming to believe that your idea of the balance actually exists for real. Note instead that these are measures of a *concept*. Of course, qualitative methods can be reliable, too, but researchers using them must be highly explicit about the assumptions that they are making in evaluating the values of their variables. If qualitative researchers do not provide the steps and ideas that underpin their assessments, they can be accused of letting their own intellectual positions affect how they have evaluated the situation. The reliability of their measures can be questioned.

Validity and reliability of variables are both very important, and you should discuss them explicitly in your section on operationalization. We have done a good amount of planning and justification, but we aren't done yet. Why? We have only operationalized our independent variable. We still need to develop a system for translating the concept representing the dependent variable—the probability of war—into an actual value. Because we cannot calculate real probabilities (the actual odds that war would occur, ranging between 0 and 1), we would likely introduce what could be called a **proxy** here, a variable that will stand in for the probability of war. What would be a suitable proxy? In choosing this proxy, we must defend its validity. Well, we might want to suggest the level of tension in the relationship as an adequate approximation of our original concept, arguing that when tensions are very high, war is more likely, and that the highest level of tensions corresponds to war and the lowest level to stability or peace. Then we still have the challenge of determining the level of tensions in a relationship. Unlike military power, we typically cannot look up figures of "tension levels" in a source book or website. Instead, we have to invent a system for determining this value. Here again, we need to find some indicators and a plan for coming to the actual evaluation of each of them. We might decide (after consulting the experts or thinking about this carefully on our own) that travel and trade, casualties from border interactions, and the way that states refer to each other and their relationship are indicators of the tensions between them. Of course, we would want to assess the validity of our measure. Then, we could plan to look up the value of cross-border travel and trade and the number of casualties in the border skirmishes in record books. But assessing the "value" of the references to each other and the relationship is a little trickier, and this is where we rely on **content analysis.**[8]

Content analysis can be done quantitatively (with numbers) or qualitatively (with words). Whichever version we choose, we must be very clear in our actual method so that another researcher could repeat our actual process and come up with the same evaluation of our measure. What content analysis does is to evaluate texts, in this case of what the government (either through documents or the words of its leaders) says and does to evaluate tension levels. (Please note: We would need to consider both actions and words, and have to have in the back of our minds that states can use both for many purposes.) In making our plan for content analysis, then, we would want to define exactly what kinds of actions and what sources of words (documents, speeches) we were going to be looking at. We would delineate these by time as well as by source (institution from which they came, speaker of the words, etc). In addition, we would have to present a system for evaluating them: What signal behaviors and words would indicate relatively low tensions? Moderate tensions? High tensions? War? Determining when the parties were at war would of course be the easiest. When we saw their armies engaged, we would know they were at war. But understanding lower levels of tension is more difficult.

---

[8]See a detailed discussion of content analysis in Janet Buttolph Johnson and H.T. Reynolds, *Political Science Research Methods,* 5th ed. (Washington, DC: Congressional Quarterly Press, 2005), pp. 222–229.

If we want to proceed in a quantitative fashion, we can seek to report the number values of travel and trade (in constant dollars) and casualties. Then, we could make a type of numeric assessment of tension through our content analysis of the words used to discuss the other state and the relationship. Here, we would determine signal words regarding the other state (friend, partner, enemy, infidel, etc.), its motives (peaceful, normal, ordinary, hostile, aggressive, warlike, etc.), and the nature of the relationship (positive, constructive, normal, hostile, enemy, etc). Then we could attach values to the words to reflect their levels of negativity. For instance, in characterizing the other state we might say that friend = 1, partner = 5, and enemy and infidel = 10. Then, we would plan to count up the references in a speech and apply the values attached to them. Higher values would then mean a more negative view of the opponent, while lower evaluations would be more positive. Alternatively, one could perform this analysis without attaching actual values, looking instead for a sense of the relationship and the view of the other from each document. Finally, our assessment of the tension level would be some sort of equation, weighting the level of travel and trade, casualties in skirmishes, and language used to come up with some figure to capture "tension level."

Using qualitative methods instead, we would get a sense of the level of tension and record that level (low, moderate, or high). Again, we would want to be explicit about how we would assess the level of tension qualitatively, to protect ourselves from charges that our measure was unreliable. Then, we would have to discuss how we would combine this assessment of language with assessments of travel and trade and casualties. We would likely come up with some evaluation—low, moderate, or high levels—for our dependent variable, tension levels. We might say that tensions are low or lessening when the amount of travel and trade between the countries is high, when there are few casualties resulting from skirmishes, and when the words used to refer to the other are complimentary or neutral. Tensions are moderate when travel and trade are at intermediate levels, there are infrequent cross-border skirmishes, and the references are relatively variable. Tensions are high when travel and trade are low, cross-border skirmishes are frequent, and the words used to describe the other are highly negative and bellicose. Please note that the quantitative measure gives the appearance of more precision because you calculate different numeric values, while the qualitative measure is expressed in different ranked and related categories.

A beginning researcher may decide to use only one indicator for tension levels, perhaps choosing from among tourism, trade, casualty, and nature of the language to come up with her measure. In making that choice, the researcher should think about both why this single indicator is a good one and what she could possibly miss by relying on only one component as she discusses the validity and reliability. After she has made her decision and defended it, she doesn't look back until her discussion in the conclusion.

After operationalizing the dependent and independent variables, we have finished the first part of the Research Design. But notice something very important: You haven't actually done any measuring yet. You do not present any values for your variables here. You determine the values in the next part of the paper, the Analysis and Assessment section. In the Research Design you present your plan, and you justify and defend it to your audience. In providing your reasoning, you should assume that your reader knows something about your topic and that she is *helpfully skeptical*. She wants you to be correct, but she's also thinking carefully about what could be wrong with your measures; your reader is a constructive critic. Thus, you should think hard about your choices and justify them carefully, but don't worry that your reader is an irascible crank. Also remember, it is rare in social science research to have "perfect" representations of your variables. You often have to make choices that are less than ideal because of resource constraints. Acknowledge these decisions and the possible problems that will flow from them, and defend them as necessary. Before moving on to perform the research, you should consider the ways in which your decision might bias your results by affecting the validity of your measure, You should return to the possibility that your analysis is tainted in the conclusion of your whole paper. But once you have determined your strategy and justified it, you can proceed without apology until the very end of your project.

DESIGNING AND SELECTING CASES

In the second subsection of the Research Design, you choose the instances that you are going to investigate. In selecting your cases, you are in essence designing your experiment. In the natural sciences and some social sciences, the preferred approach is the experimental design: Introduce a cause and see if the effect produced is what you expect. So, in chemistry you might add a particular element to your solution and see whether an explosion occurs. If you get a boom, then you are able to conclude that the element that you added caused your compound to explode. But such experimental designs are difficult to carry out in political science.[9] For instance, remembering our student researchers, Tom cannot decide to build a sports stadium in a particular place and determine its impact, nor can Kate change the institutions, economic development levels, or cultures of some countries and not others. Most of the time we cannot bring about the causes so as to see their effects, so we are left with making more choices about what instances of our phenomenon we are going to study.

The notion of "instances" or "cases" is very broad and encompasses many different factors. For the paper about Hobbes, you must decide which works of Hobbes you are going to study to evaluate your thesis. To be the most convincing, you would like to examine all of his writings so that you could see whether he consistently favored royal, absolutist rule. If you saw some variation in Hobbes' contentions, you would want to note them. Did his opinion change over time or with respect to certain issues or geographic or cultural factors? Thus, if you looked at the complete body of Hobbes' work—that is, the **universe**—then you could be convinced that you had a complete basis from which to make your conclusion.

Oftentimes it is not possible to study the entire universe of cases, every instance of a phenomenon. You may lack the time or resources. So you must select a subset or a **sample.** The goal in sampling is to choose cases that excellently reflect the whole population and introduce as little sampling bias as possible. A simple example from polling may help illuminate the bias problem in case selection and why we must be careful to avoid it.

Imagine that in late October 2000, you were trying to determine who was going to win the upcoming presidential election. To figure that out, you went to a predominantly African American neighborhood and asked the following question to likely voters: "For whom are you going to vote on election day, George W. Bush, Al Gore,

---

[9]Some research in political science does use the experimental design, however. In particular, if you were interested in the effects of debates on expected voters, you could allow voters to watch one and then interview them and see if the contest changed people's views of the candidates. Political consultants use focus groups all the time to test out ideas, phrases, and issues in a manner similar to the experimental design.

Ralph Nader, or someone else?" You would have concluded from your research that Al Gore was going to win the election in a landslide, and your research would have been terribly flawed. Why? You made a major sampling error. By questioning mostly African American voters you skewed your results. Your literature review that examined American voting behavior should have made you aware that race is an important predictor of votes. Thus, your sample needed to include cases (voters) in the proportion in which you would expect to find them in the likely voting population as a whole. To survey predominantly black voters would have a poor effect on your findings. If you were interested, on the other hand, in understanding how African Americans were going to vote in November 2000, your sample is a good one.[10]

This example underlines something important about case selection: You should keep your literature review (with both your conclusion and the *arguments that you left behind*) in mind as you try to pick the cases to study. You know that other researchers have said that different factors are important, and you want to show not only that you are correct, but that they are wrong. Therefore, you want to be sure that you are isolating the effect of your preferred cause—your independent variable—only. To do that, you typically need to *control* for other factors. When you control, you are holding these other factors constant or reducing their impact on the outcome as much as possible.

In addition, this idea of control means that you should not choose only cases that you know are "good" for "proving" your contention. In fact, expunge the words "proof" and "prove" from your vocabulary for the duration of the research project. The point in any investigation is not to *prove* but to *learn*. Would we be well-served if medical researchers always found that new drugs did what their developers said they did? No. We want to know under what conditions drugs appear to work, are ineffective or are harmful, or when the

---

[10] It is not, of course, a perfect one. You need to determine whether that person is a likely voter, because voter turnout in presidential elections is only about 1 out of 2. If you ask the person directly whether he or she is going to vote, you are likely to get the answer "yes." Most Americans know that they are "supposed" to vote to be considered a good citizen. So, to get at likelihood accurately, you may want to ask the "For whom are you going to vote" question first and then ask when was the last time the person voted. You could surmise that people who haven't voted recently or have never voted are not likely to vote this time. So their answer to the first question should not be counted if your purpose is to predict the actual percentage of African Americans voting for Gore, Bush, Nader, or someone else. For more on the importance of careful case selection, see Arend Lijphart "How the Cases You Choose Determine the Answers You Get," *Journal of Policy Analysis* 2 (1975): 131–152.

researchers still can't tell the full effects of a particular pharmaceutical. The goal of your work, like that of medical researchers, is to design a reasonable test of your argument and to report accurately what you find. Your initial ideas do not have to be right; your job here is to evaluate and investigate fairly. In this way, you learn more about the phenomenon in which you're interested.

So, in the preceding example about voting behavior, you can see that you have not controlled for race in your sample. To do so, you would need to talk to a "representative sample" of likely voters, in other words, a subset that accurately reflects the universe of cases. Professional pollsters take great pains to define their samples, and have found ways to choose only about 3000 American voters and arrive at a good estimate of voting behavior. Note, however, that even they typically identify a sampling error of plus or minus 3 percent. With a sample, it is impossible to predict perfectly, but you can get very close.

For other kinds of questions, you might need to control for some larger background factor that reflects changes occurring over historical periods. For instance, if you were looking at the effectiveness of courts in bringing about social change, selecting cases prior to 1930 would not make sense. The court's role shifted dramatically in the 1930s, and certainly after 1955, because of a larger ideational change in the United States about the proper role of the Judiciary relative to the other two branches of government. Similarly, in investigating questions of foreign policy or world politics, you might not find cases that occurred during the Cold War to be comparable to those between 1990 and 2001, or after September 11, 2001. Those historical periods reflect major differences in the structure of the international system, and you might want to keep that factor—the structure—out of your study by holding it constant, that is, picking all your cases from only one of those three periods (Cold War, 1990–2001, post-9/11).

Some kinds of questions lead to the examination of a great many cases, or what political scientists like to call "large N [for number of cases] studies." Large N studies are conducive to performing statistical analysis of the data. If you have easy access to data in numerical form, using many cases helps improve accuracy. (As pollsters' work shows, you do not need to use the universe to obtain useful results, but you need to sample appropriately.) Other questions, however, particularly ones that involve examining historical phenomena, are not going to be evaluated in the same way. Remember our hypothetical example investigating the balance of power? Suppose this hypothesis was the result of our fascination with the rivalry between States A and B and the outbreak of war between them in 1999. Well, single-case studies will allow us to generate theories but not to test them. So how can we think of this occurrence as one of a set of multiple cases in order to evaluate our theory? One way is to think of the dependent variable not simply as "war" (or "not war") but as different levels on a continuum of conflict. We've actually done that when we operationalized our concept. Then, if we conceive of the phenomenon under study as levels of tension we can include many more, very similar cases, looking at the conflict intensities over a number of years prior to (and perhaps even after) the outbreak of war. Thus, each year becomes a "case" to study.

So even if you are intrigued by and drawn to one particular incident, you should be looking for ways of making your study a comparative one.[11] Recall that Diana was interested in the 2003 U.S.-led war against Iraq. She asserted that high levels of public perceptions of the threat emanating from Iraq resulted in a highly aggressive U.S. foreign policy toward that state. To confirm that perceptions of extreme threat explain bellicose foreign policy and estimations of less danger account for more moderate responses, she decided to examine American anti-proliferation policy toward North Korea, too.

The North Korea case is a good one to pair with Iraq, not only because the nature of the U.S. response was so different, but also because the reality of nuclear proliferation in that East Asian country hit the headlines in late 2002, at the same time that the Bush administration was making its case for war against Iraq. Thus, this juxtaposition allows Diana to look at very different outcomes of the dependent variable while holding other factors (such as the distribution of power in the international system, the American administration, and the key political constituencies of that leadership) constant.

But what if Diana believed that these two cases weren't a good pairing? She might contend that the strong suspicion that North Korea had useable nuclear forces meant that the power positions of Iraq and North Korea were too different. Her reasoning could be that the United States would be deterred from acting against a (potentially) nuclear North Korea, and not against Iraq. So, to find comparable situations, Diana would not look to the American response to North Korean proliferation efforts, but instead would break down the U.S.-Iraqi relationship into time periods. Thus, a "case" could

---

[11]Arend Lijphart, "Comparative Politics and the Comparative Method," *American Political Science Review* 65 3 (September 1971), 682–693.

become a month in time over the course of, say, 1992 until June 2003. For each case she could determine the perceived level of threat and the aggressiveness of the American response. Then Diana could use statistical analysis to see whether her hypothesis held over these many cases. If Diana were overwhelmed by this task (determining the value of these variables across more than 132 months), then she could shorten the time span (maybe from 1997 to 2003). Still, she would be examining a large number (N) of cases, and with this amount of information she would be able to use statistics to evaluate her hypothesis.

What if, however, there was no way that Diana wanted to use statistics in her research paper? For whatever reason, she wanted to perform a historical case study. She still cannot study just one case if she wants to evaluate a theory. Diana needs to perform at least a comparative case study[12] where she examines how well her independent variable can explain widely varying outcomes (at least two) on the dependent variable. Or, if Diana can't find enormously different levels of the effect (levels of aggression), then she should look at what happens when she maximizes the variation in her cause (extreme differences in the perceptions of threat). Diana could then find a way to select two or more time periods in U.S.-Iraqi relationship after the 1991 Gulf War that would allow her to compare historical cases when either causes or outcomes are very different. Finding cases that are comparable and maximize variation in one of her variables produces a good test for Diana's hypothesis.

The point of this discussion, then, is that even when you think there is only one case that you can study, there are ways to generate at least one comparative case. First, you can divide the instance into two (or more) time periods, looking for one in which the incidence of either the dependent or independent variable is highest and another where one of them is lowest. This maximizes the variance of either the dependent or independent variable, allowing you to evaluate your hypothesis at the extremes. A second strategy is to find another comparable case (with controls of other possible causes in place) in which either the outcome (aggressiveness) or cause (threat perceptions) are very different. Again, the goal here is to introduce disparity in the variables and determine whether you can still sustain your hypothesis. More than one case helps build confidence in your findings, and even if you are not going to investigate hundreds of cases,

---

[12]Alexander L. George and Andrew Bennett, *Case Studies and Theory Development in the Social Sciences* (Cambridge: MIT Press, 2004).

you can still make a comparison that will allow you to understand better the relationship between the variables and, thus, the appropriateness of your hypothesis.

IDENTIFYING DATA SOURCES

The third part of the research design is to identify what information you are going to use *to measure your variables* and exactly where you are going to get it. But this is not a section in which you provide an annotated bibliography for your paper. The focus here is in finding the information that you need to evaluate your hypothesis. For example, if you were working on the argument linking the balance of power to the probability of war, you need to identify precisely where you are going to find military spending, armed force size, and WMD holdings for states A and B (in order to calculate your independent variable, the balance of power), plus travel and trade flows, casualties from border skirmishes, and language used to discuss the other in official statements and documents (to determine the proxy for your dependent variable, the level of tensions). The reason to identify your sources now is to make sure that your plan for determining your variables is actually workable. If you can't find this information, you need to come up with an alternative method for operationalizing your concepts.

When you are identifying your sources, you should not simply take information from any place that you can find it. You want to be sure that you have the *best* source, given your constraints. Please do not perform a "Google" search and take information off of any website that you find. If you have no idea who the source is, leave that data alone. Look for alternatives from reputable sources. Otherwise, readers will not take your findings seriously, as they might doubt the accuracy of your information. Remember that if your data is problematic (i.e., invalid or unreliable) your analysis will be flawed. To locate the best possible sources, look first to scholars who are interested in questions similar to yours and see where they have found their data. Then, you can feel more confident in your choices. Other times you might just know that your source has a fine reputation. For instance, if you're interested in the attitudes of ordinary Americans on social issues of the day, you can consult the General Social Survey conducted by the University of Michigan. Or if you need basic demographic data about the U.S. population, you can consult the U.S. Census Bureau. Information about money in American politics (who gives and receives) is available at www.opensecrets.org. There are many reputable sources of opinion data around the world, with EuroBarometer being an excellent one surveying the citizens on Europe. The Freedom House also ranks the countries of the world on a seven-point scale on the levels of freedom and liberty (both concepts defined). Great sources for military data are the Stockholm International Peace Research Institute's *Yearbook,* the United Nations, the International Institute for Strategic Studies' *Military Balance,* or the CIA *Factbook.* Lastly, the World Bank's World Development Indicators are a wonderful source of information on political, social, and economic conditions throughout the world. These are just a few examples of well-known and excellent data sources. For the kinds of information mentioned, there is no need to look anywhere else. A little searching for your particular question should help you find the "right" sources too. If you're having trouble identifying them, go see the reference librarians at your institution. They will be enormously helpful to you.

Even when you pick excellent, well-respected data sources, you can have questions about their figures. Sometimes even the best organizations can't get precise data. For instance, in our example of studying the conflict between States A and B, and the role of the balance of power, we have to recognize that some states— particularly countries that are non-democracies and whose spending decisions are therefore not accountable to the population— do not report their figures accurately. In providing figures for these kinds of states, our trusted sources sometimes make decisions about what to report: They may list the actual figures that these governments release or they may provide their own estimates. So, if you are dealing with one of these types of states, you might want to note this potential problem or even come up with a different indicator of state power for it. Still, no one expects you to go out and determine these figures for yourself. You work with the best that you have, noting the potential problems with validity, and you move on.

You may think consulting your data sources now, when you are only making your plan for your research, is premature, but it is a crucial step in the Research Design section. By looking for data now, you make sure that what you hoped you could get—as you defined in your first two subsections—is actually available for the cases you want to study. In effect, then, specifying your data sources here and checking that they actually have what you need ensures that your wonderful plans for evaluating your argument are actually possible. If you can't get access to the information that you need, then you might have to modify your earlier strategy, and it's better to know that now rather than later.

To underline the importance of checking out your information sources at this stage, let's revisit two of our examples. Thinking about our investigation of the conflict between States A and B, if we can't find information about travel and trade flows or casualty levels resulting from border skirmishes, then the only indicator that we can pursue is the perception of the other reflected in the language used. We would then have to adjust your operationalization plan accordingly. Or imagine we were investigating the way in which ideology affected people's attitudes toward the 2003 Iraq War. You had originally wanted to argue that ideology was a nationally important indicator of popular attitudes on this war, and you assumed that the major polling organizations routinely asked—from August 2002 until November 2004—respondents their opinion toward the war *and* about a person's ideology. When you actually tracked down the polls, however, you found that these organizations did NOT ask about ideology. They might have only asked the question "Do you (or would you, if the query was posed before March 2003) support the war against Iraq?" Now that you know the information you were hoping to use isn't there, you have some choices to make. Are you going to keep the case selection (general U.S. population) the same or are you going to look at a different sample? You could decide to change the sample, looking at some local subset at the current point in time only—people on campus, people in a nearby community— and design and perform the survey yourself to get at your precise issue. Or you could decide to keep your case selection (national over a two-year period), but introduce a proxy variable for ideology. Obviously, you would want to define your proxy based on what data existed to choose from (i.e. what pollsters *had* asked). Thus, if the polls provided party identification you might use it as a proxy for ideology and consider the extent to which it closely represents ideology. You would need to include a discussion of the possible weaknesses of this measure as a proxy. (Is this a valid measure? What are its limitations?) If you find that this approximation for your preferred factor is not strong enough, you may decide to go back and change your thesis under investigation (party affiliation → attitudes), noting that "the data made me do it!" As long as you explain what you are doing and why (and these points are logical and accurate), you are safe from criticisms that your work is poorly conceived.

STRATEGIES FOR UNCOVERING AND, AT TIMES, CREATING DATA

For some of you, after you have operationalized your variables, picked your cases, and found your sources, you'll be ready to move on to the Analysis and Assessment of your thesis. For others of you, however, there is still one more step. There are times when the operationalization of your concepts means that you have to come up with ways for uncovering and, in a sense, generating data. I hesitate to use the word "create," because I do not want any reader to think that you just make up your information to suit your purposes. But while operationalizing often means conceiving (or re-conceiving) of your variable as a factor for which data can be easily found (i.e., GDP figures, poll data for a certain time period, election results, or military spending figures), or even producing some sort of a composite out of indicators, at other times you are going to have to come up with an additional strategy for generating raw information, which you will then have to transform into useable data.

Typically this occurs when the data or information doesn't exist in any central location because you are applying a thesis to a new area or application or you are looking at some very current problem. In those cases, you might need to develop a survey or an interview questionnaire so that you can amass the information that you need. Remember, any time you plan to perform research on human subjects you need to receive permission from your institution's research board. So, you will need to design this instrument and submit it to both your professor and that board for approval. In writing the survey or interview, you, the author, also face many questions. Two very important ones are (1) Should it be open-ended or should I give respondents answers to choose from? and (2) How long should it be? Other concerns involve the very careful writing of the questions so as not to confuse, mislead, or suggest an answer to any of the participants in the study. Here you must pay close attention to reliability (meaning that neither you nor whoever is administering the instrument is *eliciting* particular answers) as well as validity (the questions you are using to generate information are a good translation of the variables in your model).[13]

In sum, whenever you need to develop a method for generating information, you must explain exactly what you are doing and how you are doing it. In addition, you must set out the logic behind your approach, justifying every decision that you made as the best one for accomplishing the task at hand given the resource constraints under which you are operating.

FINISHING TOUCHES ON THE
RESEARCH DESIGN

You have now become acquainted with the tasks you need to accomplish in the Research Design. As you write up this section, remember that it should be able to stand alone as an essay, yet be integrated into the rest of the text. Consider this the section in which you explain exactly how you are going to conduct your research and why your research strategy will help you answer your question as accurately as possible. Thus, the section answers the query: How should I proceed for the truest assessment of my thesis? It should be set off from the rest of the text with a heading, and include introductory and concluding sections. The body of the essay must accomplish the three tasks identified at the start of this chapter.

This is one section where the generic title, "Research Design," may be the most appropriate. Or you could come up with a more creative heading. Just be sure to use some title to set this section off from the rest of the paper. In addition, because you must perform the three or four rather involved tasks—concept definition and operationalization, case selection, data identification, and, if necessary, information generation—you also might want to use subheadings.[14] Thus, you need to be aware of how to indicate subheadings given the particular format that you are using. In *Chicago Manual of Style,* for instance,

---

[13]Many research methods textbooks provide excellent advice on designing surveys and performing interviews. See for example, Janet Buttolph Johnson and H.T. Reynolds, *Political Science Research Methods,* 5th ed. (Washington, DC: Congressional Quarterly Press, 2005), pp. 270–304.

[14]You may want to use sub-headings in other sections, too. Typically, the longer a section is, the better a candidate it is for subsections.

headings are communicated by centering the title and typing the letters in uppercase. The next level of sub-heading, then, is left justified and underlined.

Let's look at how Matt, our student investigating the continuing relevance and appropriateness of the Electoral College, handled the challenge of the Research Design.

ELECTORAL COLLEGE RESEARCH MAP

The discussion of this normative topic will be divided into four sections, in which four questions will be asked as a way to isolate the key aspects of the debate. First, what was the thinking behind the development of the Electoral College? Through the writings of the Framers and the scholarly work of historian Forest McDonald, a basic understanding of the original intent for the Constitution— as well as the logic behind the document and why it was designed as it was—will be achieved.[15] The Framers' intent, logic of the Constitution and the debate between the Federalists and Anti-Federalists help define the "American civic religion." Second, how is the Electoral College a good representation of these foundational American ideas? Third, what is American nationalism and what is the role of such nationalism in a system in which power is divided territorially and some is reserved for states. The tension between citizen empowerment and state-level influence is important here as several scholars, including Longley and Braun, Zeidenstein, and Dahl, explain.[16] Finally, what is the intersection of federalism and nationalism, and how does this point showcase what America is and how the Electoral College is representative of the essence of the US? Taking all four criteria into consideration, the Electoral College will emerge clearly as a key American institution and a fundamental element of the civic religion.

Because Matt's paper is normative, he is setting out principles that he needs to investigate to arrive at an assessment of his claims: the

---

[15]Forest McDonald, *E Pluribus Unum: The Formation of the American Republic 1776–1790* (Boston: Houghton Mifflin Company, 1965).

[16]Lawrence D. Longley, and Alan G. Braun, *The Politics of Electoral College Reform* (New Haven: Yale University Press, 1972), Harvey Zeidenstein, *Direct Election of the President* (Lexington, MA: Lexington Books, 1973), and Robert Dahl, *How Democratic Is the American Constitution?* (New Haven: Yale University Press, 2002).

Electoral College is consistent with American traditions and should remain as the method for deciding U.S. presidential elections. Here, he contends that four points are essential for evaluating this contention. He spells them out and details some of the sources that he will use in assessing each. At the end of his section introduction, he presents the reader with his conclusion, setting out a logic as well as his findings.

Matt has a good first start on his design. What he still needs to do, however, is defend the choices that he makes. Why, exactly, are these four key issues? Why did he choose some scholars and not others? He must answer these questions to defend against claims that he has introduced bias into his analysis. Thus, even normative papers need to describe the validity and reliability of measures. Be sure that you include that explicit discussion in your paper.

PRACTICAL SUMMARY

The Research Design is the section of the paper in which you provide the plan for your research—how to define and operationalize the concepts, choose cases, identify information sources, and, sometimes, generate data. Typically, you cannot define or conduct a true experiment to evaluate your hypothesis, so you have to make well-informed choices about how to proceed. As long as you are aware of the concerns about methods—minimizing bias, controlling for other explanations, choosing cases that maximize variance in either the dependent or independent variable—you can come up with a "good" plan. Such a program, however, is likely not to be perfect, so you must be explicit about the possible imperfections and their effects on your research. You will return to consider how the choices that you made about the design affected your analysis in the concluding section of the research paper.

To write the research design, I suggest that you proceed as follows:

1. Develop an introduction that answers the general question "How am I going to conduct the research for this project?" with special attention to (a) the delineation and measurement of concepts, (b) case selection, (c) the specification of information sources, and if necessary, (d) a strategy (when necessary) for generating data.

2. In the first subsection, discuss precisely how you will translate your concepts (independent and dependent variables) into

knowable entities. This is often a multi-step process. For evaluating a contentious statement, you have to provide careful definitions of these terms and specify steps that will show how you will know when the parts of your argument are sustained by the evidence. When analyzing a hypothesis, you might have to find indicators or even proxies for your variables. You may even have to determine how multiple indicators will combine to create your final "value." After determining this plan for coming up with an assessment, explicitly address the validity and reliability of your "measures" and recognize that "measures" are not necessarily numbers.

3. In the second subsection, decide what cases you are going to study. Be sure that you are choosing a sufficient number to evaluate your argument effectively. Also, you must be concerned with controlling for other possible causes when you pick your instances. If you are performing empirical research and are going to use statistical techniques, you must have more than 30 cases. If you are performing a historical case study, you must find a way to make this analysis comparative. Find another case (either by dividing your preferred case into periods that differ because of varying outcomes on the dependent variable or by finding another incident that is comparable) to study. When you are not using the universe of cases, beware of introducing bias into your study by sampling. And remember: Your goal is *not* to prove your thesis but to evaluate it.

4. In the third subsection, identify the data sources that you will use to help you determine the "values" of your key concepts or variables. Be sure that each of these is reputable. Do not simply "Google" to find some information on the Internet. You must be sure that the source of the information and the data itself are trustworthy. If you cannot get access to the data that you wanted, you need to re-think the decisions that you made in the first and second subsections.

5. If necessary, include a fourth subsection that clearly specifies how you will generate data that do not exist. If you need to design an interview questionnaire or survey, describe the goals for writing it and any concerns you had in developing the instrument, and include a copy of it as an appendix to the text. Also, fill out the necessary paperwork and submit this questionnaire to your institution's review board for approval.

6. Write a conclusion that specifies the choices that you made, acknowledges potential problems that may result from these choices, and suggests that after you perform the analysis you may have to revisit the significance of these decisions. However, you are now ready—with your plan established—to proceed with the evaluation of your argument.

7. Remember, this section provides the plan and justifications for your work only. The actual evaluation of the variables and the discussion of the relationship occur in the next part of the paper, the Analysis and Assessment Section.

SUGGESTED CALENDAR

About halfway through the course, you should begin developing your plan for your study. I cannot stress enough how important it is for you to determine whether what you have proposed is workable. In other words, you must see whether actual data exist to carry out your design or whether you can find or generate the information that is essential for your study. Too many students do not look carefully at their plan until involved in the next stage, the Analysis and Assessment, and realize to their horror that they have not put together a workable proposal or (even worse but frequently the case) that they really have no plan at all. Please do not think that this planning process is simply a "make-work project." It is actually central to the success of your study, so take it seriously and work through all aspects of it—operationalization of dependent and independent variables, case selection, source searches, and data generation—at the halfway point. That way, you will have the time to adjust your plan if necessary, and not be left in the last few days before the paper is due with a completely unworkable and nonsensical project.

EXERCISES

1. Operationalize the concepts for the any two of the following arguments:
    - In the United States, the courts are not as effective an instrument of social change as are legislatures.
    - Hard-line leaders are more likely to succeed in achieving peace or rapprochement with enemies than are soft-liners.

- Women should wield political power at a level comparable to which they exist in a population.
- The greater the threat to U.S. national interest, the more aggressive the U.S. foreign policy response.
- Republicans are far more likely to support the 2003 Iraq War than are Democrats. Independents are less likely than Republicans, but more likely than Democrats to favor the war.

Evaluate the validity and reliability of your measures.

2. Determine the cases for assessing any two of the following theses:
   - In the United States, the courts are not as effective an instrument of social change as are legislatures.
   - Hard-line leaders are more likely to succeed in achieving peace or rapprochement with enemies than are soft-liners.
   - Women should wield political power at a level comparable to which they exist in a population.
   - The greater the threat to U.S. national interest, the more aggressive the U.S. foreign policy response.
   - Republicans are far more likely to support the 2003 Iraq War than are Democrats. Independents are less likely than Republicans, but more likely than Democrats to favor the war.

   Explain how your case will provide an excellent and fair test for your thesis.

3. Using actual resources, identify data sources for any two of the studies you have already begun designing in numbers 1 and 2 above.

CHECKLIST FOR THE INTRODUCTION, TITLE, AND RESEARCH DESIGN

Below is a checklist to consult while you are writing and before you turn in the second installment of your research paper. Fill it out accurately, and any time you cannot check off an item, go back and address the problem. If you have proceeded as recommended, at this point you are writing a first draft of your Introduction, Title, and Research Design, and revising your Literature Review and Model and Hypothesis sections based on the earlier comments you have received or ideas that have emerged as you have continued working on the project. When you turn in this installment, the sections should appear in their proper order: Title (actually, title page), Introduction, Literature

Review, Model and Hypothesis, and Research Design. As before, the checklist identifies the essential elements of the new sections and indicates that you should have gone back and tackled any problems that you or your professor identified with earlier sections of your paper. Again, you can see that writing issues figure prominently here.

Substantive Concerns for the Introduction and Title

1. Does your Introduction communicate your research question succinctly, clearly, and in an interesting way? Is the puzzle easily identifiable?   _____

2. Have you effectively explained why this question is interesting and important to political scientists, policy makers, and ordinary citizens?   _____

3. Have you provided a "road map" for your paper, including a sentence or two summary of each of the sections?   _____

4. Does your title communicate the puzzle, cases, and argument in as clear and as memorable a way as possible? Would *you* look at something with that title and say enthusiastically, "I'd like to read *this!*"   _____

5. If your title is "catchy," is it still appropriate for a formal writing assignment? Is its meaning clear to the average reader?   _____

Substantive Concerns for the Research Design

6. Have you written introductory and concluding paragraphs for the Research Design section? Have you developed and included an appropriate heading (title) for this section?   _____

7. Does your section introduction "introduce" by explaining the purpose of the section and providing the reader with a "road map" to this section?   _____

8. Have you developed an actual plan for operationalizing your concepts (i.e., measuring your variables)? (This plan explains exactly what steps you will take to "know" the value

of your variables.) Does your plan seem reasonable and workable? Have you included a discussion in the text about the validity and reliability of your measures? (Have you really *thought through* this discussion?) _____

9. Have you picked cases that allow you to evaluate your hypothesis by maximizing the variance in either your dependent or independent variable? Are you looking at the universe of cases or a sample? Have you controlled for other explanations (or held other possible causal factors constant)? Have you included a discussion in your Research Design section that explains why you've made the choices you have? _____

10. Have you identified your data sources? Are they primary sources? If not, why not? _____

11. If you are "generating" data by coming up with a plan for content analysis or writing a survey or conducting interviews, have you attached in an appendix the actual plan, survey, or interview questions? _____

12. Does your section conclusion "conclude" by explaining why the choices you made are the best ones for your purposes? _____

Fixing Installment 1

13. Have you addressed all of the comments and issues that your reader has raised on the first installment? _____

14. Have you addressed all of the concerns that *you have* about the first installment? _____

Writing and Formatting Concerns

15. Have you properly cited the sources of your ideas? Have you avoided plagiarism? Do all your citations conform to the appropriate format? _____

16. Because the Introduction, especially, is a place to
    establish your own voice, have you avoided long
    quotes (except, perhaps for an epigraph) there
    and in the Research Design?   _____

17. Have you run the spell and grammar check,
    remembering that these functions are not foolproof? _____

18. Have you numbered your pages, but not the
    title page?   _____

19. Have you included a bibliography that conforms
    to the format specified?   _____

20. Recognizing the limits of spell and grammar check,
    have you edited your paper?   _____

21. Add your own personal writing concerns. (By now you should
    have a very specific personal list.)
    - split infinitives   _____
    - sentence fragments   _____
    - run-on sentences   _____
    - good transitions   _____
    - word choice/overuse of words   _____
    - homonym confusion   _____
    - overuse of pronouns   _____
    - passive voice   _____
    - length of paragraphs (more than a sentence, less
      than a page)   _____
    - other   _____

7

Evaluating the Argument: The Analysis and Assessment Section

Y ou're more than halfway through the research-paper writing mar-athon, and you are feeling pumped because the course is now downhill and there's a wind at your back. The fun part of the project is about to begin; you are ready to investigate the actual phenomenon in which you are interested, and all the work that you have done so far will help guide and protect you during this evaluation. Your thesis and research design will direct you: They have defined precisely what you need to evaluate and exactly how you are going to perform this assessment. The careful work of your Research Design also will guard you against charges that you have introduced bias into your project.

Briefly, there are two main forms of *analysis*—**qualitative** and **quantitative.** The major distinction between the two approaches is the use of words versus numbers as the main form of evidence. With qualitative analysis, an investigator assesses evidence or facts in the form of words to determine where the weight of it lies—on the side of the thesis or against it. With quantitative analysis, the evaluation of the thesis is primarily on the basis of numeric information. A researcher rejects a hypothesis because the numeric data shows that the relationship that he posited among the variables is not statistically significant. In other words, the researcher makes a calculation that allows him to throw out or accept his thesis.[1] Oftentimes, however, researchers combine qualitative and quantitative forms of analysis in their work, so do not be surprised to see a mixture, too.

Regardless of which type of analysis you pursue, you need to remember that (1) your thesis or model and hypothesis allows you to concentrate on what is important and (2) your research design specifies exactly what you need to do. In other words, the analysis section is where you keep a laser-like focus on your argument and what you need to do to assess it. Though you might be enticed to add additional, interesting, yet extraneous information, resist that temptation! That tendency is an old habit developed from your "report writing" days. Now you are beyond that; you know that a research paper consists of the careful analysis of a thesis, not simply a broad story about some political event, phenomenon, or idea. To put yourself in the proper mindset for this section, think back to the many courtroom dramas that you have seen. The Analysis and Assessment section is the trial phase of your research project. You've done the background work, and now you are ready to present your case. What do lawyers do at the trial? They present the logic of their argument and then the evidence that supports their interpretation of events. They do not, for instance, recount all the details of the various interviews they conducted prior to their date in court or bring witnesses to the stand that do not add something substantial to their case. So, if you're writing a paper on the Supreme Court confirmation process since 1973, it is irrelevant to discuss the names of the spouses of all the candidates who have gone before the Senate Judiciary Committee since that time. In this section of the paper, like the attorney, you are going to lay out the facts that you have collected that are pertinent to your argument. Unlike the lawyer, however, you should have no vested interest in whether your case holds or not. Remember, an

---

[1]Note that with statistical analysis, there is always some probability that the relationship that you find to be significant is not. If we accept a hypothesis at the 99% confidence level that means there is still a 1% chance that this relationship has occurred by chance.

important difference between you and the attorney is that *you are not an advocate* for a position, but an investigator in search of knowledge.

QUALITATIVE ANALYSIS

Political Science undergraduates are most likely to be familiar with qualitative analysis. Many of us become interested in Political Science because we like reading newspaper, magazine, or policy articles that make arguments (predominantly based on logic, values, and historical evidence) about political ideas or phenomena. Most of the readings you have done in your introductory courses and even many of your upper division classes (especially in Political Theory, American Politics courses on the presidency, urban politics, the bureaucracy, the courts, and many topics in International Relations and Comparative Politics) primarily use qualitative analysis. But what is this as a form of analysis? Isn't it just description and argumentation? Yes, there are descriptions and arguments included in these assessments, but remember that the assessment is focused, concentrating on the thesis and employing the methods that you set out in your research design.[2]

Let's think back to some of the theses that we have seen before and consider how to assess them. Let's start with two that are contentious statements but are not concerned with exploring the interconnections between the factors.

- Hobbes is an opponent of liberal associationalism; he defends and supports royal rule. He is, therefore, not a forefather of liberalism as some have contended.[3]

- Religion was (and should continue to be) central to the formation of the American government and governance. The American identity is (and should continue to be) Protestant.[4]

Imagine that Boyd and Huntington had not already written their pieces guided by these very theses, and that you want to assess these

---

[2]An excellent resource on a form of qualitative analysis, case studies, is Alexander L. George and Andrew Bennett, *Case Studies and Theory Development in the Social Sciences* (Cambridge: MIT Press, 2004).

[3]Richard Boyd, "Thomas Hobbes and the Perils of Pluralism," *The Journal of Politics* 63 (2001), pp. 392–413.

[4]Samuel P. Huntington, *Who Are We? The Challenges to America's National Identity* (New York: Simon & Schuster, 2004).

arguments. What would you do? You might initially think that you should go back to your literature review—which explores these debates—and see what the evidence is that others have cited and then decide with whom you agree more. NO! In a research paper, you are supposed to perform your own analysis. In a sense, you are putting yourself on the same level as those scholars and asking, "What do I think, based on the evidence?" You are going to do original, creative work.

But how exactly do you do this analysis? As we discussed in Chapter 6, to sustain the first argument, a student would have to have very clear definitions of "liberal associationalism," "defense and support of royal rule," and "liberalism" and she would have a plan for assessing Hobbes' stance on these points. In the Analysis section, the student follows through on her plan. She studies her cases (in this instance, the texts of Hobbes that she decides to sample) and determines how Hobbes really felt about these positions, based on her assessment plan. To what extent does he reveal opposition or support? The student would likely want to amass all the **evidence** that she found from carefully reading Hobbes' texts to show (a) his opposition to a vibrant civil society and (b) his defense and support of royal rule. For this thesis, evidence would consist of quotes from Hobbes that discussed the evils or problems inherent in the formation and activity of social groupings and the importance of maintaining sovereign authority vested in a single, special individual. In other words, the actual data sources for evaluating these contentions are Hobbes' own words; the text is the data in a Political Theory paper.

There is an additional point in this thesis that has to be substantiated: Hobbes is not a forefather of liberalism. To address that contention, the writer would want to explain and discuss liberalism. Here, she could consult her courses in Political Theory as well as scholars of liberalism. From these experts, she would cull a definition of liberalism. In order to sustain her hypothesis, she would want to show that Hobbes' positions on the role of groups in society and the value of monarchical authority make viewing him as a forerunner of that school impossible. The student would have to determine whether the bulk of Hobbes' language and argument showed that her contention could be sustained rather than that of the opposing school of thought (that liberals can trace their intellectual lineage back to Hobbes).

In writing this (and any) Analysis and Assessment section, the student needs to walk the reader through her investigation in a step-by-step fashion. Thus, she would be well-served to use the major points of the argument as the subsections, working through the elements one at a time, providing all the corresponding evidence relevant to each part. So she would have three subsections: (i) Hobbes' view of societal groups, (ii) Hobbes' affection for royal rule, and (iii) the importance of associationalism and distrust of monarchs in liberal thought. Under each of these subsections, the researcher explains the logic and presents the facts, again like the lawyer making her case in court. She writes her narrative, relying on key quotes from Hobbes and explaining how the evidence convinces her to reach her particular conclusion.

Of course, we must remember that all the information may not support the student's original contention. If that occurs, the student need not worry, but will have to consider the extent to which her argument holds. Qualifying her claims may be necessary, if she finds, for instance, that the evidence supports that Hobbes rejects only a particular element of liberalism or if she finds that his ideas developed over time. The point is that the student needs to report accurately what she learns about her thesis. Whatever her findings are, she still contributes to the debate on Hobbes, making her stand—based on what the evidence shows—regarding his place either as a forefather or opponent of liberalism, or something in-between.

The second argument about the place of religion in the founding of America and in contemporary society, is both empirical (what was) and normative (what should be).[5] In providing evidence to support the empirical contention, a student would rely on the cautious specification of these concepts and then go to the Founding to assess religion's role there. This work would require a careful reading of key documents from the early period, as well as letters and diaries of the Founders, congressional debates, and executive and judicial acts from the first few decades of the republic. The data are the words of the Founders and governmental acts. As in the analysis of the first thesis, the student here would have to read texts very closely and amass the weight of the evidence on the basis of the themes and arguments made in these sources.[6]

The second part of this thesis, however, requires a different form of assessment. The normative element requires persuasive, value-laden argumentation to convince the reader that (Protestant) religious identity is essential for the proper functioning of the United States. Here, the student would want to be explicit about the values that he was privileging

---

[5]Note that Huntington actually traces the importance of religion beyond the Founding period, but for simplicity's sake, we will assert that this thesis addresses only that early time.

[6]Notice that a student could apply either qualitative or quantitative content analysis to either of these tasks.

and explain why these are more important than others. In addition, he would need to show that only by maintaining a Protestant religious commitment could the same, preferred outcome be achieved. To win over skeptics and opponents, the student would be well-served to anticipate counter-arguments and show why they were logically and/or normatively flawed. Thus, in this paper, the assessment portion would be both empirical and normative. The argumentation would be based both on extensive knowledge of facts (regarding the Founding) and a commitment to particular ideals that the student defends as the "best" ones (a Protestant religious identity) for achieving the most desired outcome (a well-functioning American democracy).

In sum, the analysis of the thesis requires conceptual clarity and careful examination. But how do you actually perform this assessment? Again, we can turn to an example to see how a real student handled this task. Remember Matt's research design for assessing the utility of the Electoral College? Back in Chapter 6, Matt told us that he would assess the logic and development of the U.S. Constitution to determine (1) the essence of the "American civic religion," (2) the College's place as an embodiment of this religion; (3) the nature of American nationalism; and (4) the central importance of federalism to the American civic religion and politics. As Matt proceeded, he defined the civic religion as embodying the commitment to empower both citizens and states. Then, in asserting the College's essential role in translating this idea into practice, Matt wrote the following subsection:

THE ELECTORAL COLLEGE AS THE EMBODIMENT OF THE CIVIC RELIGION[7]

The Electoral College and the rest of the Constitution were not miraculous creations that developed through divine intervention; they were born out of practical considerations and intense debate. Indeed, the debate behind the Electoral College is analogous to the whole federal convention. Three election scenarios were advanced: direct election by the people, an Electoral College (similar to the College of Cardinals in the Vatican), and the election of the chief magistrate by the national legislature.[8] The direct election option was the least

---

[7]Note that this title is a subheading within Matt's Analysis and Assessment section. That is why it is left justified and not centered and in uppercase as full section titles are.

[8]Philip B. Kurland and Ralph Lerner, eds., "Article 2, Section 1," *The Founders' Constitution,* vol. 3 (Chicago: University of Chicago Press, 1987), pp. 536–44.

popular, and it was discounted by the likes of James Wilson of Pennsylvania for two reasons: he believed that an election would create a dangerous situation, citing the difficulties involved in selecting a Polish magistrate, and that it would be impossible for a majority to be created among the people.[9] These were very real fears in 1787, especially with insurrections like Shay's Rebellion as well as the lack of communication and ability to know enough about a national candidate. . . . The idea of having the national legislature choose the executive was shelved for fear that the president would become too beholden to the members of Congress . . . The Electoral College plan seemed to be the compromise between direct election and election by the legislature. It had the virtue of representing local interests—which a direct election would guarantee—while at the same time tempering local issues with truly national ones. Moreover it would have the final check of politically non-affiliated but knowledgeable electors voting for president. . . .

This excerpt provides you an example of how Matt sought to assess the second essential point of his argument. He turned to the actual debate at the time of the Founding, and later, in a part of his discussion that I did not include, to the contemporary scholarly assessment of the College's role to uphold his contention.

Qualitative analysis is useful for assessing hypotheses, too, although it works best for the analysis of a few cases.[10] Typically, you would use qualitative analysis to investigate a few different historical or geographic instances of the phenomenon in question. For instance, Diana sought to understand why the United States would invade Iraq and not North Korea in 2003. She contended that these cases were comparable because at approximately the same point in time both states were trying to develop weapons of mass destruction in violation of international commitments and norms. She claimed that public perceptions of threat explained the differences in policy. Americans, in the era of Islamic terrorism, believed that Iraqi attempts to build the bomb were the greatest danger that the United States faced. The North Korean nuclear program fell off the radar screen, thanks to Administration efforts to link Iraq to *al Qaeda* and to press the Iraqi threat to the American homeland. Thus, in analyzing U.S.

---

[9]*Ibid.*

[10]Again, see George and Bennett for guidance.

policy, Diana looked at how the perceived levels of threat from Iraq increased over the course of 2002 to 2003, whereas the public sense of the menace emanating from North Korea was much lower. The variations in these societal assessments of peril accounted for the differences in U.S. action according to Diana.

In sum, when performing qualitative analysis, focus on the thesis to guide you through your analysis. Use the plans you developed in the Research Design to perform your evaluation, and when you write up your findings in the Analysis and Assessment section, carefully walk through the elements of the thesis as you determine what the information reveals. Upholding one's thesis is *not* the goal. The accurate and unbiased evaluation of the evidence is.

COMBINING QUALITATIVE AND QUANTITATIVE ANALYSIS[11]

My experience with Political Science majors shows that more than half of all of them have no desire to perform quantitative analysis. Closing our eyes to the value of numeric data is short-sighted and closed-minded, however. While there are highly sophisticated forms of statistical analysis that one can use to assess political phenomenon, many approaches and techniques are within reach of all Political Science majors, particularly now that so many of the calculations are performed automatically by programs to which students have easy access.

Students can employ numeric information to great advantage in analyzing their hypotheses, without having to resort to using complex statistical analysis. Let me provide one fictional example to illustrate this point. In the last chapter, we looked at how to operationalize the concepts in the hypothesis that the more that power is balanced between two states, the less likely is war to erupt between those countries.[12] Imagine that you wanted to investigate that hypothesis for the

---

[11]While some might assert that before I look at how to combine qualitative and quantitative analysis, I should introduce students to quantitative analysis, I choose to introduce the different kinds of analyses from least quantitative to most. My logic for doing this is my experiences with my own students. The more numbers I present to them, the more frightened (and sometimes closed minded) they become. Thus, I'm trying to offer smaller amounts of numerical information first, in the hope that I will build confidence in the ability to use numbers and allow students to develop an appreciation for quantitative analysis.

[12]This line of reasoning would follow from the balance of power hypothesis formulated most notably by Hans Morgenthau in *Politics Among Nations*.

TABLE 7.1 Military Holdings of A and B (Dollar Values and Numbers of People are Provided in the Millions. Spending Data Reported in Constant (1999) Millions of Dollars)

	State A			State B		
Year	Defense Spending	# People in Military	WMD Holdings	Defense Spending	# People in Military	WMD Holdings
1990	400	.385	5	300	1.2	0
1991	410	.387	5	302	1.2	0
1992	388	.353	5	250	1.1	0
1993	192	.310	5	151	1.1	0
1994	200	.320	5	155	1.1	0
1995	300	.320	5	155	1.1	0
1996	320	.350	10	190	1.1	0
1997	350	.350	10	220	1.2	0
1998	375	.400	15	280	1.2	0
1999	400	.450	20	350	1.2	0

situation that emerged between two countries, A and B. These two states share a common border. In 1992 the countries had finalized a nonaggression pact, and in 1999, State B attacked State A. Do changes in the balance of power help us understand the changes in the relationship between these two countries?

In Chapter 6 we detailed our plan for assessing this hypothesis over a ten-year period (1990–1999). We decided that to calculate the balance of power we would first need to assess the military strength of each state. We contended that strength was a function of the amount of money spent on defense, the number of people in the military, and the levels of weapons of mass destruction that each possesses. Thus, our first job would be to find these figures for the years in question. To operationalize the variable and make the process as transparent as possible, we would want to go to one or more of those reputable sources for military data that we had identified in our research design and then present this information to the reader in a table like Table 7.1 (please remember that the scenario and data reported here are fictional).

Next, we remember that these figures are the components of strength, but we still need to determine the balance. We could do this quantitatively or qualitatively. To be transparent, we would remind

TABLE 7.2 Measures of the Balance of Power

Year	Quantitative	Qualitative
1990	1.338[13]	Slight advantage A
1991	1.362	Slight advantage A
1992	1.556	Slight advantage A
1993	1.281	Slight advantage A
1994	1.300	Slight advantage A
1995	1.938	Increased (v. 1994) advantage A
1996	1.706	Slight (less than 1995) advantage A
1997	1.609	Slight advantage A
1998	1.368	Slight advantage A
1999	1.176	Slight (less than 1998) advantage A

the reader of our equation or logic and then present the results in another table. Recall that the formula for the balance was

Balance

$$= \frac{0.3 \times \text{mil spending in A} + 0.5 \times \text{force size of A} + 0.2 \times \text{A's WMD holdings}}{0.3 \times \text{mil spending in B} + 0.5 \times \text{force size of B} + 0.2 \times \text{B's WMD holdings}}$$

Insights similar to those that inform this equation affect the qualitative assessment. If proceeding qualitatively, we would remind the reader that in coming to our assessment of strength, we believe force size is most important, followed by military spending (as an indicator of the quality of the forces), and then the level of WMD. Our comparison of strength levels would give us a sense of the balance.

Of course, we would only pursue one approach (the numeric or the word-based) to measuring our variable in our paper, but I am providing the results from both methods here (Table 7.2).

After presenting this table (or actually one half of *this* table, since we would only be showing either the quantitative or the qualitative measurements), we should interpret it for the reader. If we were proceeding with a quantitative assessment of the balance, we might want to include the following text: "The data show that at the outset, the power that B possesses is almost the same as that of A. In other words, military might is very close to being balanced, as the ratio of A's holdings to B's is almost one. Throughout the decade the power positions are nearly identical, and the balance fluctuates very slightly,

---

[13]The results were calculated with the help of Excel and rounded to three significant digits.

with A's advantage rising to its highest relative position in 1995. Thereafter, the power differential falls until it is the closest to being balanced in 1999. Interestingly, this is also the year that the states went to war with each other." On the other hand, if we were performing qualitative research we might want to say something like the following: "The data shows that at the outset State A has a power advantage (the greater spending and nuclear weapons help to put it in a better position), but it is a small one (since the size of B's military is significantly larger). This situation (slight advantage for State A) held through 1994, and then A undertook steps to increase its power, tipping the balance somewhat more in its favor. B responds to these moves, however, and by the end of the decade, the distribution of power is only slightly out of balance and not very different from what it was in the first year of our analysis."

This evaluation of our independent variable helps me make three important points. First, tables, charts, graphs, or other pictorial representations of information are excellent additions to your data analysis section. These are devices for briefly summarizing important information for your reader's consideration, and they help you see the data in a nutshell. Remember, a picture (or even a table) is worth a thousand words in your Analysis and Assessment section, even if you are performing qualitative analysis. Sometimes patterns can jump out at you in a table or a chart in a way that they do not when you have to read through multiple pages of description to learn the full story. The second point, however, is that the writer should interpret and provide the significance of this summary of data for the reader, highlighting patterns and stressing the important developments. Third, these summaries can serve as a kind of outline for your section, as you can see the important transition or changing points that you need to discuss and explain.

Still, with all the work that we have done to uncover this information, we only have half the story. The hypothesis has two parts:

Part 1: the greater the imbalance of power

Part 2: the more likely is war

All of the information presented so far is focused on understanding the extent to which power is balanced (the independent variable). None of that tells us about the dependent variable—the likelihood of war. In Chapter 6, we decided that we would use a proxy—the level of tensions—between A and B and determine that proxy using three indicators. Let us say that we followed the steps set forward for a qualitative assessment and found (and presented) the following (Table 7.3):

TABLE 7.3   Levels of Tensions between A and B

1990	Moderate tensions
1991	Moderate tensions
1992	Lower tensions (than 1991)
1993	Moderate tensions (increase over 1992)
1994	Moderate tensions (about same as 1993)
1995	Moderate tensions (about same as 1993)
1996	Crisis—increasing tensions
1997	Increasing tension (worse than 1996)
1998	Increasing tension (worse than 1997)
1999	War

We could then summarize our findings on our independent and dependent variables by presenting both of these tables, but our work would not be done. We would then want to ask, "Does the hypothesis hold? Does that statement (the more power is balanced, the less likely is war) help us make sense of ten years of this relationship?" In assessing the hypothesis, we would probably want to provide a single table that combines these findings, as well as a narrative that carefully explains what happens to the dependent variable (likelihood of war) when the independent variable (balance of power) changes. Again, the table could be a *part* of the research paper, but it would not provide sufficient analysis. Whether we include the table or not, by writing it down we have an outline for the assessment of the hypothesis: the measures capture much of what was happening. (Note again: if we were actually performing this analysis in our paper, we would not provide both a quantitative and a qualitative assessment of the balance. Because we have determined both here for illustrative purposes, I have chosen to include both. See Table 7.4.)

This numerical data gives us some sense of what was going on with the balance of power, but it might not provide us with the whole story. We should also read about these state's military holdings and ambitions so that we can see what is happening to affect the level of the tensions between the two parties. Remember, our hypothesis didn't simply assert that the variables were *correlated*—that greater imbalances of power would occur *at the same time* that tensions increased—but that there was a *causal relationship* between them—shifts in the balance would *affect* the levels of tension. Thus, we need to uncover the story of why the shifts in the relationship occurred. In

TABLE 7.4 Balance of Power and Likelihood of War (Combining Tables 7.2 and 7.3)

Year	State of the Balance Quantitative	State of the Balance Qualitative	System Tension Levels
1990	1.338	Slight advantage A	Moderate
1991	1.362	Slight advantage A	Moderate
1992	1.556	Slight advantage A	Lower
1993	1.281	Slight advantage A	Moderate, > 1992
1994	1.300	Slight advantage A	Moderate, = 1993
1995	1.938	Increased (from 1994) advantage A	Moderate, = 1993
1996	1.706	Slight advantage A (less than 1995)	Increasing
1997	1.609	Slight advantage A	Increasing, > 1996
1998	1.368	Slight advantage A	Increasing, > 1997
1999	1.176	Slight advantage A (less than 1998)	War

this section of the paper, you want to engage in what Alexander George called "process tracing," telling the "story" of how changes in the balance of power affected the probability of war breaking out between A and B. If the impact of the balance of power on tensions is high and works across a number of years, then we could conclude that we sustained the hypothesis.[14] Thus, we need to provide our reader with information that is not captured in this table. Is it really the balance of power that is affecting the probability of war?

Imagine if your exploration of the level of tensions found that the reason they increased in 1996 was that State A announced that it was going to enhance its nuclear arsenal, and in 1997 the International Atomic Energy Agency issued a report stating that State B was illegally attempting to develop nuclear weapons, in violation of its commitment to the Nuclear Non-Proliferation Treaty. These developments speak directly to the idea that the balance of power has an effect on the level of tension and the probability of war in the system. But what if the source of the crisis was that a new governing party was elected in

---

[14]See George and Bennett, *Case Studies and Theory Development in the Social Sciences* (Cambridge: MIT Press, 2004), especially Chapter 1. Process tracing is also very useful in pure qualitative analysis.

State B, one with a racist ideology that defined citizens of State A infe-rior? Thereafter tensions increased as State A responded with its own hateful statements regarding State B and was found responsible for fund-ing a group in State B that was engaged in a separatist struggle. Do these actual developments help sustain a balance of power argument?

My point here is that the basic "value" of these variables tells you something important, but they may not explain the whole context in this situation. The table helps provide an outline for you regarding the direction of the variables and their values over a period of time. Then, your job is to investigate whether your particular hypothesis holds and the reasons for the increase in the level of tensions is important. You must discuss this in your analysis. This example shows us that often analysts combine quantitative and qualitative data to assess their hypotheses. You may have begun this study thinking that you would perform a traditional, qualitative analysis of this question. However, some of the data that is very useful comes in the form of numbers. You can and should use these figures to have a better under-standing of your concepts and ultimately your hypothesis. Ultimately, though, you evaluate the hypothesis using both qualitative and quan-titative methods to provide a complete assessment.

QUANTITATIVE ANALYSIS

As many of you expected, much of quantitative analysis deals primarily with statistical analysis. However, this method of investigation neither has to be boring nor difficult to a student interested in politics. As we have already noted, statistical analysis is particularly useful for assessing highly general contentions, ones that can apply to many cases. When you begin contemplating quantitative analysis, you need to (a) identify what kind of data you will be using—continuous or discrete—and (b) be sure you have sufficient cases (more than 30) to make the stat-istical analysis valid.

Remember the following hypothesis:

Republicans are more likely than Democrats to favor the 2003 Iraq War; Independents and nonaffiliated Americans are more likely than Democrats but less likely than Republicans to view the war favorably.

What type of information is involved here? To evaluate this hypoth-esis, you would be putting people into categories, reflecting both their party affiliation and their attitude toward the war. As these are both discrete measures, you would be looking to use a Chi-Square statistic to determine whether the distribution of results occurred due to chance or whether party affiliation actually had an impact.

To test this hypothesis, imagine that you decided to conduct a survey of students on your campus. In compiling your data, you were allowed to survey virtually all freshmen in the social sciences.[15] You asked them to provide some basic demographic information and then asked them to check off answers to the following:

I consider myself a:
Republican   _____
Democrat   _____
Independent/Other _____

My attitude toward the 2003 Iraq War is
Favorable   _____
Unfavorable   _____

Your results were as follows:

		Party Affiliation			
		Republican	Independent/ Other	Democrat	Total
Attitudes Toward 2003 War	Favorable	90	40	40	170
	Unfavorable	10	10	60	80
	Total	100	50	100	250

What do these tallies mean? To determine a meaning you want to compare your matrix of **observed values**—the information above that you gathered or observed—compared to a matrix of *expected values*. (A matrix is simply a two-dimensional chart that reports figures in rows and columns. In this format, you should typically display the independent variable across the top for the columns and the dependent variable along the side for the rows.) The expected values are those that you would expect if the independent variable (party affiliation) had *no impact* on the dependent variable (attitudes). In other

---

[15]You might choose this sample because it is one to which you could get easy access at your school. In your Research Design section, you would want to discuss the significance of using this sample, of course, and consider what impact it could have on your findings.

words, you want to compare what you found through your survey with the "null hypothesis," the outcome that you would see if there were no relationship. So if party affiliation were irrelevant, then Republicans, Independents/Others, and Democrats would each feel the same way about the war. When there is no relationship, then knowing a person's party affiliation tells us nothing about how he or she feels about the war. If, on the other hand, party affiliation does explain attitudes, then we would expect to see differences in the way the people from the parties feel about the war. And that distribution of attitudes across parties would be varied.

While we may be able to discern a pattern simply by looking at the results, we can calculate the precise nature of the relationship by using something called the *Chi-Square statistic*. This statistic will tell you the extent to which your observations are different from what you would expect to see if there was no relationship between the independent and dependent variables. Moreover, if the results are significantly different, then the statistic will let you know at what *confidence* (or *probability*) *level* you can uphold your hypothesis. In other words, if your statistic holds at the .01 confidence level that means that you can be 99 percent sure the results that you found could not have occurred by chance. In other words, you can be 99 percent sure that you have found a relationship between your independent and dependent variables.

There are a number of *statistical packages* that will perform this computation for you. (A statistical package is a software tool that comes ready to perform all sorts of functions as long as you supply the data and tell the program exactly what you want it to do.) Below, I use *SPSS,* very easy to run now that it is a Windows-based program. There are many other packages that you can use, so feel free to employ one with which you are already familiar or the one that your professor recommends. Notice, also, that you can compute the χ^2 (Chi-Square) statistic yourself. Because I think it is useful for you to see and understand the simple mathematics involved, I'm going to present the arithmetic here. Hopefully, seeing the process broken down will also give you a better intuitive sense of what the statistic is trying to capture. To calculate χ^2 for our example, note that

Observed value$_{i,j} = O_{i,j}$
Expected value$_{i,j} = E_{i,j}$
N = total number of respondents, 250 for our example

Note: i refers to the row number
    j refers to the column number

In this example, $i = 1$ or 2 (favorable or unfavorable) and $j = 1$, 2, or 3 (Republicans, Independents and Others, or Democrats). Note that the totals are not counted "officially" in your matrix, but they will be important in your calculation. That is why I included them above.

Thus, for example, $O_{1,1} = 90$ (90 Republicans favored the war) and $O_{2,3} = 60$ (60 Democrats responded unfavorably to the war)

So, if $i = 1$, and $j = 1$,

$$E_{1,1} = \frac{\text{Total of responses in row } i \times \text{Total of responses in column } j}{N}$$

$$E_{1,1} = \frac{(170 \times 100)}{250}$$

$$E_{1,1} = 68$$

We can continue making calculations for the whole matrix until we arrive at the following:

Expected Values (if there were no relationship between party and attitude)

$E =$		R	I/O	D
	Favorable	68	34	68
	Unfavorable	32	16	32

Then you calculate the Chi-Square statistic in the following manner:

$$\chi^2 = \sum \frac{(O_{i,j} - E_{i,j})^2}{E_{i,j}}$$

where "Σ" means the sum of all the values, from $i = 1$ to 2 and $j = 1$ to 3

"O" Matrix—Observed Values			"E" Matrix—Expected Values		
90	40	40	68	34	68
10	10	60	32	16	32

Calculations (rounding to 3 decimal places):

$$\chi^2 = (90 - 68)^2/68 = (22)^2/68 \quad = \quad 7.118$$
$$(40 - 34)^2/34 = (6)^2/34 \quad = \quad 1.059$$
$$(40 - 68)^2/68 = (-28)^2/68 = 11.590$$
$$(10 - 32)^2/32 = (-22)^2/32 = 15.125$$
$$(10 - 16)^2/16 = (-6)^2/16 \quad = \quad 2.250$$
$$(60 - 32)^2/32 = (28)^2/32 \quad = 24.500$$
$$\chi^2 = 61.642$$

The number that you computed ($\chi^2 = 61.642$) is a statistic that you need to compare to those in an already-generated reference table to see whether you have found a significant relationship. But there is one more calculation that you need to make before you can look in the table: You must determine the **degrees of freedom** (DoF) for your example. This number reflects the size of the matrices with which you have been working and the number of categories you are examining. Intuitively, the more cells that you have in each matrix the greater could be the size of the Chi-Square statistic, since you would be summing more values. But degrees of freedom is not simply the number of cells; instead it is as follows:

$$\text{DoF} = (\text{rows} - 1) \times (\text{columns} - 1)$$
$$= (i - 1) \times (j - 1) \qquad \text{or in this case}$$
$$= (2 - 1) \times (3 - 1)$$
$$= 1 \times 2$$
$$= 2$$

Now you turn to the table and look up under 2 degrees of freedom the value of Chi Square at different levels of significance. You find that at 2 degrees of freedom, the Chi-Square values are the following:

Confidence Levels[16]	.1	.05	.01	.001
DoF 2	4.605	5.991	9.210	13.816

The value for Chi-Square in this example— 61.642—is greater than any of the values shown in this table at 2 degrees of freedom. That means that the relationship that you have found is significant at greater

---

[16]Anthony Walsh and Jane C. Ollenburger, *Essential Statistics for the Social and Behavioral Sciences: A Conceptual Approach* (Upper Saddle River, NJ: Prentice Hall, 2001), Appendix A, Table 5, 281.

than the .001 level, or that you can be confident 99.9 percent of the time that party affiliation is an excellent predictor of attitudes toward the 2003 Gulf War. In this case, the numbers are overwhelmingly good. But imagine that we had different outcomes and the χ^2 came to 8.97. What would that mean? Well, this figure is greater than 5.991 (.05 level in the table at 2 DoF) and less than 9.210 (.01 level in the table at 2 DoF). Thus, this statistic holds at the .05 confidence level. If you had calculated a χ^2 of 8.97 you would explain that you can accept this hypothesis—that party affiliation predicts attitudes— at the .05 level. Your predictions would be correct 95 percent of the time. If, however, your Chi-Square calculation were 4.41, then you would have to reject your hypothesis. In the social sciences, we typically sustain a hypothesis if it holds at the .1 level or lower. We don't want to accept an argument that is wrong more than 10 percent of the time. That level (greater than 10%) of inaccuracy is unaccept- able. So, if you calculated a 4.41 χ^2 for a set of data in a 2x3 table you would have to conclude that party affiliation does not adequately pre- dict attitudes toward the Gulf War.

The χ^2 is useful in evaluating relationships between sets of discrete data (remember, information that comes in categories), but there are other tools to use when understanding the relationship between con- tinuous or interval data (information that spans a continuum). The last type of quantitative analysis that we will consider is what is called a *Simple Linear* or *Ordinary Least Squares (OLS) Regression.* Please note that there are other statistical tests that you can use. I am simply dem- onstrating one that I have found useful for my students.[17] You should consult a reference book and/or ask your professor as you determine precisely what type of statistic you should calculate. OLS will evaluate whether your independent variable affects your dependent variable in a predictable way, represented by the following mathematical equation:

$$Y = a + bX$$

Where Y = dependent variable (effect)
$\quad\quad\quad X$ = independent variable (cause)
$\quad\quad\quad a$ = intercept of the line along the x-axis
$\quad\quad\quad b$ = slope of the line

Again, while there are other types of regression that you can perform, we are going to assume that a linear relationship is adequate for many types of research that beginning students will be evaluating.

---

[17]See Walsh and Ollenburger for other tests.

Remember Kate and her project investigating the hypothesis that the higher the levels of economic development, the higher the percentage of women in politics? Recall also that in her literature review, Kate found that culture might be another important explanatory factor. So to test her assertion, she decided to control for culture, picking a subset of states with similar values. Then, Kate began collecting data on economic development, deciding to use GDP per capita values because many studies linking development to democracy use this as a proxy for development.[18] To assess the level of women in politics, Kate also decided to examine the percent of women in the national legislature. Suppose she gathered her data and found the figures summarized in Table 7.5 (note that I have created this data for illustrative purposes). Now Kate's job is to make sense of this information. What she would like to determine is whether the level of women in the parliament is a function of economic development. To do that, she uses a statistical package, such as SPSS, to run a linear regression.

In this case, Kate wants to run a regression because she has two continuous (or interval) variables and she wants to see if they are related. What regression analysis does is fit a line through the points, not by connecting the dots, but by capturing the trend of the direction and slope of the data. Then, the program computes a statistic called the R Squared which tells us something about how close the line is to the actual data. When R^2 is 1, then the calculated line fits the data points exactly. The R^2 tells us the amount of variation in our dependent variable that our independent variable explains. As R^2 decreases, it shows our independent variable as less powerful in accounting for the dependent variable. In other words, the closer that R^2 comes to zero, the worse the line fits. For a low R^2, one very close to zero, the points are either scattered throughout the diagram with seemingly no pattern to them or arrayed in a band around a horizontal line (one with zero slope). If we see no pattern, then we can guess intuitively (and see visually) that the independent variable has no effect on the dependent variable. Also intuitively, when our eye can see a line (assuming we're performing a linear regression) then we are likely to find a relationship when we have the package perform the calculation. In the social sciences, an R^2 of .4 (an R of about .63) is decent. If our calculations give us those values, then our cause explains 40 percent of the variance of our effect.

---

[18]Seymour Martin Lipset, *Political Man: The Social Bases of Politics* (Baltimore: Johns Hopkins University Press, 1981) and Adam Przeworski and Fernando Limongi Neto, "Modernization: Theories and Facts," *World Politics* 49, no. 2 (1997): 155–183.

TABLE 7.5 Development Levels and Percent of Women in Parliament

Country	Economic Development Level ($GDP PC)	% of Females in National Legislature
1	20,000	15
2	15,000	25
3	25,000	20
4	22,000	22
5	28,000	33
6	29,000	8
7	18,000	11
8	17,000	9
9	24,000	18
10	30,000	32
11	31,000	38
12	13,000	14
13	15,000	15
14	14,000	12
15	19,000	10
16	23,000	21
17	33,000	5
18	31,000	25
19	26,000	20
20	28,000	6
21	21,000	28
22	17,000	10
23	11,000	8
24	13,000	10
25	14,000	12
26	34,000	35
27	37,000	30
28	14,000	15
29	15,000	12
30	13,000	8

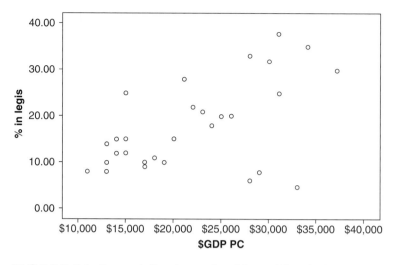

FIGURE 7.1 Economic Development and Percent Females in Parliament

So, first let's use SPSS to perform a **scatterplot** of this data. A scatterplot simply is a graphing of the data. Here, the x-axis is our independent variable—GDP per capita—and the y-axis is our dependent variable—percent of women in the national legislature. Let's look at our graph.

Just looking at the graph in Figure 7.1, we can note a few things. You can probably eyeball an upward sloping line here, although there are some important outliers (particularly the three data points of low levels of women in the legislature when the GDP PC is between $28,000 and 33,000). Still, looking at the scatterplot tells us there is likely some positive relationship (because the line we can imagine "best fitting" is *upward* sloping). Now let's actually compute the line and see what the R statistic tells us.

Using SPSS again, we can run the regression to find the equation for the line as well as the value of the R^2.

Model Summary

Model	R	R Square	Adjusted R Square	Std. Error of the Estimate
1	.551[a]	.303	.278	7.99024

[a]Predictors: (Constant), $GDP PC

ANOVA[b]

Model	Sum of Squares	df	Mean Square	F	Sig.
1 Regression	777.734	1	777.734	12.182	.002[a]
Residual	1787.632	28	63.844		
Total	2565.367	29			

[a]Predictors: (Constant), $GDP PC
[b]Dependent Variable: % in legis

Coefficients[a]

Model	Unstandardized Coefficients		Standardized Coefficients	t	Sig.
	B	Std. Error	Beta		
1 (Constant)	2.676	4.509		.594	.558
$GDP PC	.001	.000	.551	3.490	.002

[a]Dependent Variable: % in legis

As you can see, SPSS provides us with a lot of information. What is most important for our purposes is to look at two of these key statistics. The first is the R^2 value. As we can see, $R = .551$ and R^2 is .303. This means that economic development levels explain 30.3 percent of the variance in the levels of female representation in parliament, leaving 59.7 percent explained by other factors. While there is a relationship between GDP and female representation levels in parliament, there are other important determinants, too.[19] We should note that when using other kinds of data—for instance, survey data—we

---

[19]Students with more training and interest in statistics would want to note the following: Another useful statistic, the "F" statistic, evaluates whether the line that we calculated through these points is significant. And here, with a "Sig" or significance level of .002, we can say that yes, our line is significant. And what is this line? To determine the line, we look under the coefficients and see that we have values calculated for the intercept and the slope (a and b, respectively, in the equation $y = a + bx$). The line for this equation would be $y = 2.676 + .001x$. We need to note that our intercept is not significant, while the slope is (at the .02 level, or 98% of the time.) In addition, after running this regression, a student might want to scale the values for economic development levels, relating thousands of dollars of GDP to percentages. (In other words, for country 1, the economic development level would be 20 instead of 20,000.) By rescaling, the R value would be the same, but the slope would be calculated to .687. Prior to scaling, the slope was .000687, which got converted to .001 with rounding.

would be more likely to find lower R^2 values. Individual behavior is much harder to predict than country behavior, as individuals have so many different reasons for acting the ways they do (as psychologists will remind us).

After you have performed the regression, it is important to look again at the scatterplot to see if you can gain any further insight. Look at the points that are far removed from the trend – this is called "residual analysis." In this case, we might want to look at those three points clustered at low levels of female representation and very high levels of economic development. Perhaps further analysis would show us that these three countries had only recently experienced a huge increase in economic development levels compared to the other wealthy countries in the sample. That might allow us to assert that there may be a lag time between economic development and female electoral success. Or maybe, looking at these countries again, we saw that we might have been a little too lenient in including them in our sample because they were culturally distinct from the rest of the cases in a few definable ways. That would reinforce our commitment to controlling for culture.[20]

In writing her Analysis and Assessment section, Kate would want to include a table presenting all of her data, as well as the computer-generated results (including the scatterplot). Then she would need to interpret the results for the reader, writing a paragraph or more to explain what these computations mean for her hypothesis. She should also engage in residual analysis and perhaps perform a second regression, excluding the questionable data points. If she does that, she again should show the statistical analysis that her package produces and interpret the meaning of these computations for her hypothesis. Through all this she must remember that not upholding her hypothesis is fine. Kate is not graded on whether she had the correct best guess, but whether she performed proper and careful analysis, interpreted her results correctly, and presented them in an effective manner.

In sum, when performing quantitative analysis, you make calculations (often with the help of computers), but then it is up to you to interpret the results for your reader. Moreover, you are well served to collect as much data as you think might possibly be relevant (keeping in mind the alternative arguments that you found in your

---

[20]If Kate had more data points, she might want to eliminate those outlying cases and recalculate her statistics.

literature review) to help you better understand the relationships that you are observing and to perform controls.

Hopefully, this foray into quantitative analysis shows you that numbers and statistics are highly useful and can be very interesting to political scientists as figures help us better understand (or ask more questions about) political phenomena.

FINISHING THE ANALYSIS
AND ASSESSMENT SECTION

The Analysis and Assessment section of the paper is where you have the opportunity to tell the "story" of the phenomenon that piqued your interest in the first place. In general, the best approach to telling that story is to break the thesis or hypothesis down into its parts. If you have only a few comparative cases, you may want to designate each case as a major section and follow this advice within each section. Divide the Analysis and Assessment into subsections, each focusing on how you have actually evaluated a particular key concept in your argument. Then determine where the weight of the evidence falls on your thesis. Can you sustain it? If your thesis has multiple parts or concepts, to what extent does the evidence sustain each of your contentions? If you are performing empirical analysis of a causal argument, organize the analysis around the determination of the independent variable, the dependent variable, and then an assessment of the causal connection. Can you uphold your hypothesis?

As you write up this section, you want to make sure that it can stand alone as an essay that answers the following questions:

1. What is the evidence or data on your thesis?
2. What do the data suggest about the veracity of your argument?
3. Why is this so?

In addition, you want to be sure to come up with an appropriate title for this section and consider using sub-headings to divide the section into parts, particularly if you are evaluating different hypotheses or performing residual analysis. Your section should also have introductory and concluding paragraphs. Within the section, you want to be sure that you present evidence and information in ways that are clear and easily accessible to the reader. Whether you are using qualitative or quantitative analysis, including a summary chart of the evidence is an excellent idea because it focuses the reader's attention on the precise argument as well as the weight of the data. Many students using qualitative analysis will be surprised to learn that they *can* develop a summary chart; it is not simply a technique for numerical information. Also remember that regardless of which type of analysis you choose, your text—your explanation and interpretation of the evidence—is extremely important in walking the reader through the information and what it all means. You must remember to stay closely focused on your argument when you write your narrative. You may feel a pull toward telling the reader everything you know about a particular phenomenon. But the "everything-but-the-kitchen-sink" approach to analysis and assessment is counterproductive. The reader only wants (and needs) to know the extent to which the evidence supports your preferred argument. Thus, you don't want to lace your assessment with lots of extraneous facts. Note that in your Analysis and Assessment section you will have many footnotes to the sources of your data (where you actually found the "raw information"— whether it is from texts, statistical handbooks, speeches, your own surveys and interviews), but the interpretation of it should be all your own. No one has performed this precise analysis before, and you are explaining what it all means.

PRACTICAL SUMMARY

The Analysis and Assessment section of the paper is where you decide whether (and sometimes to what extent) you can sustain your argument. You make this decision based on evidence that you carefully assemble according to the method you set out and the sources you identified in your Research Design. You should not feel compelled to reach a positive finding. Social and natural scientists are constantly learning by being wrong about what they originally thought. What is important is that you accurately assess your contention using appropriate data. Depending on your research question, the type of information that is available, and the number of cases that make sense to study, you will perform qualitative or quantitative analysis. (Sometimes, you may be able to mix the two.) Regardless of which you employ, you want to amass evidence carefully—looking at all sides of the argument and, where appropriate, assessing the relationship between the variables. Remember not to get distracted by extraneous information. Also, while other experts may have interesting opinions on related subjects, what is most important for you is to develop your own set of evidence and interpret its meaning on your own, without the help of those scholars. Thus, your evidence should come from "raw" data—information that has not already been interpreted in texts, statistical handbooks, speeches, or from your own surveys and interviews.

To write this section of the paper

1. Write an introduction that sets out briefly the weight of the evidence for your argument and what this information means for your thesis.

2. Begin assessing the argument by examining the first part of your contention or the independent variable. If possible, present the information in a summary chart and then write a narrative explaining the meaning and significance of this data. You would likely be well-served to treat this as a separate subsection with its own title. (If you are performing empirical analysis, and you have more than one independent variable, write a subsection/s that presents the evidence for each variable.)

3. Continue with your assessment by investigating the second part of your contention or the dependent variable. Try to present this information in a summary chart, too. Then, if you are investigating an empirical thesis, determine whether the independent variable really affects the dependent variable by engaging in process tracing (for qualitative analysis or a combination of qualitative and quantitative) or statistical analysis.

4. Throughout the presentation and analysis of your evidence, remember to stay focused only on the argument that you are assessing. Do not include extraneous information that will confuse the reader. Also remember that your job is not to "prove" your contention, but to evaluate your argument.

5. Write a conclusion that explains what you found and why.

SUGGESTED SCHEDULE

Ideally, you should be working on your Analysis and Assessment Section throughout the second half of the course. Your goal should be to finish a first draft of this part with sufficient time left (about two weeks) to write your Conclusion, as well as to revise and edit your whole paper. Check with your professor regarding his or her precise timing recommendations.

EXERCISES

1. Go back to the hypothesis and data provided in this chapter regarding the situation between states A and B. Write the text of an Analysis and Assessment section for a research paper that explored that relationship and the stated balance-of-power hypothesis.

2. Consider the hypothesis and the data provided linking party affiliation and attitudes toward the 2003 Gulf War. Write up an Analysis and Assessment section for a research paper that explored that hypothesis and had amassed that data.

3. Consider the hypothesis and the data provided linking levels of development and female representation in parliaments. Write up an Analysis and Assessment section for a research paper that explored that hypothesis and had amassed that data.

CHECKLIST FOR ANALYSIS
AND ASSESSMENT

Following is a checklist to consult while you are writing the third installment of your research paper. Fill it out accurately, and any time you cannot check off an item, you need to go back and address the problem. If you have proceeded as recommended, at this point you are writing a first draft of your Analysis and Assessment section, and revising everything that came before based on the earlier comments you have received or ideas that have emerged as you have continued working on the project. As before, the checklist identifies all the key elements of this new section and indicates that you should have gone back and tackled any problems that you or your professor identified with earlier sections of your paper. Again, you can see that writing issues figure prominently here.

Substantive Concerns for the Analysis
and Assessment

1. Have you written an introduction to this section that sets out briefly the weight of the evidence for your argument and what this information means for your thesis? Does this introduction to the section provide a road map for the section? _____

If You're Using Qualitative Analysis

2. If you are performing qualitative analysis and looking at a few cases (i.e., a few occurrences of the particular phenomenon you're interested in), have you organized your discussion and description by case? Thus, if you were investigating the hypothesis that the balance of power explains the different levels of U.S. aggressiveness toward Iraq and North Korea, do you have two subsections, one explaining the Iraqi case and the other explaining the North Korean case? _____

3. In these case studies, have you used your hypothesis and research design to guide you? In other words, is your historical discussion focused on determining what was happening to the independent variable and the subsequent values (in words) of your dependent variable? Have you used your method for operationalizing the variables that you set out in the Research Design to guide you in determining the "values" of these variables? (So, for the hypothetical example, do you focus first on what was happening to the balance of power and at the same time how aggressive the United States was toward Iraq? Then, in the next section, you focus on the balance of power and how aggressive the United States was toward North Korea?) _____

4. If possible, can you include a chart to summarize what was happening over time to both your independent and dependent variables by using words? _____

Or If You're Using Quantitative Analysis

5. Have you used your hypothesis to guide you in this section? _____

6. Have you followed the method that you set out in the Research Design to determine the values of your independent variable? Are these provided in a chart for the reader? _____

7. Have you followed the method that you set out in the Research Design to determine the values of your

independent variable? Are these provided in a chart for the reader? _____

8. Have you included additional charts or graphs to present the information most effectively (e.g., an observed values matrix for a Chi-Square or a scatterplot for a regression)? _____

9. Have you explained what the meanings of any statistics that you (or a computer) calculated are? Have you included a discussion of whether your hypothesis holds or not and how you know that? _____

Fixing Installment 2

10. Have you addressed all of the comments and issues that your instructor has raised on the second installment? _____

11. Have you addressed all of the concerns that *you have* about the second installment? _____

Writing and Format Concerns

12. Have you properly cited the sources of your ideas? Have you avoided plagiarism? Do all your citations conform to the appropriate format? _____

13. Because the Introduction, especially, is a place to establish your own voice, have you avoided long quotes (except, perhaps for an epigraph) there and in the Research Design? _____

14. Have you run the spell and grammar check? _____

15. Have you numbered your pages, but not the title page? _____

16. Have you included a bibliography that conforms to the format specified? _____

17. Recognizing the limits of spell and grammar check, have you edited your paper? _____

18. Add your own personal writing concerns. (By now you should have a very specific personal list.)
   - split infinitives _____
   - sentence fragments _____

- run-on sentences   _____
- good transitions   _____
- word choice/overuse of words   _____
- homonym confusion   _____
- overuse of pronouns   _____
- passive voice   _____
- length of paragraphs (more than a sentence, less than a page)   _____
- other _____   _____
- other _____   _____

8

Considering the Significance and Limitations of Your Findings: The Conclusion

When you make it to the Conclusion you are in the home stretch of your race and you want to finish strong. You are a few miles from the finish line, the crowds are cheering, but you have hit "the Wall." You're exhausted, and you feel as if you can't run any more. Like the marathoner in the last few miles, you are likely very tired after completing the Analysis and Assessment, but you are not finished yet. You must run these last miles; finish this crucial section of the paper. If the Introduction is your first impression, the Conclusion is your last one, and you want it to be highly positive. You want to race, not limp, across the finish line, right? Just like a fine dessert that caps off a wonderful meal, you want your Conclusion to leave your reader feeling satisfied.

Your Conclusion accomplishes several different tasks. First, it ties the whole paper together by restating your thesis and where the weight of the evidence came down. Second, the Conclusion discusses why the argument and the particular findings (across your cases) are important and what your results mean for various audiences. Third, it assesses the versatility of your thesis, considering the extent to which you can apply your argument to other cases or, conversely, whether you need to limit its applicability. Fourth, the Conclusion is a critical assessment of what you accomplished. Here, you return to those "best decisions" that you made in the Research Design section and consider what impact they had on your findings. What, if anything, would you do differently if you could do this study over again? Lastly, the Conclusion is a jumping-off point for the future, for you or other researchers who might like to pick up where you left off. This is where you can set out questions to pursue to continue this line of research in a fruitful manner.

As you know by now, the research paper consists of at least four different sections prior to the Conclusion (Introduction, Literature Review, perhaps Model and Hypothesis[1], Research Design, and Assessment and Analysis). When you first started writing this paper, you probably could not adequately conceive of how these sections were related to each other and what the logical flow between them was. At this point, you have hopefully mastered the interrelationship between the segments and through your section introductions and conclusions have helped to provide smooth transitions between the different parts of the paper. The Conclusion also helps you accomplish this task by tying the paper together one last time for the reader (and the writer): briefly reminding the reader of what your question was, why it was important, what you thought the "best" answer to that question was, how you were going to evaluate this contention, and what the assessment of the evidence showed. The concluding section briefly walks the reader through the significance of the research, the argument, and the evidence.

An extremely important part of this discussion is to remind the reader why anyone should care about what you found. Why was your research question so important? Why are the instances that you studied significant? Remember, you want to answer these

---

[1]This section is often not necessary for a normative question or a noncorrelational or noncausal argument. See Chapter 4 for details.

questions from the perspective of several audiences. For the social scientific community, your findings say something about a theoretical debate in the field. Remind your reader of the scholarly controversies and what you have learned about the merits of a particular line of reasoning. In addition, your results also have significance for the interpretation of a particular set of cases. For practitioners, your findings might provide advice about appropriate behavior when dealing with comparable cases, and for citizens, your work might be important for understanding the world or being "better" members of a local, national, or global community. Normative work provides the added benefit of enlightening us about what ought to be and how we ought to behave.

Your Conclusion probably engenders feelings of both pride and humility. As you consider what you did and what you found, you should think about the extent to which your findings provide insight into other cases. Take pride if your results help you understand any other political phenomena. But perhaps you need to scale back your earlier claims, finding that your thesis only partially applies or is relevant to a smaller subset of cases. Consider whether some of the limitations may have resulted from faulty decisions you made at earlier stages in the research (Literature Review or Research Design), and you could never recover from those choices.

Thus, while the Conclusion requires that you wrap this paper "package," you should not feel that the tying has to be "neat" and that once "tied" you are done with your discussion. In fact, research is often quite messy, and despite our best efforts to find uncomplicated support for our original contentions, we often cannot reach such a "nice" conclusion. Remember, you do not have to prove your assertions; you simply need to evaluate them honestly. This section is where you come back to the compromises and the lines of logic you pursued—whether you found support for your thesis or not—to consider whether your choices had both a significant and possibly a detrimental impact on your study. In the Conclusion, you might want to suggest that a different school of thought appears stronger now or that you would alter the research design (whether in operationalizing the variables, selecting cases, choosing sources, and/or generating information) in certain ways. Of course, you should explain why you want to make these changes, as well as assert why you think these modifications would lead to a "better" study.

Finally, regardless of how tired you are with this research, you should discuss at the end how you would proceed if you had the resources (and the stamina) to continue. In doing this, you reinforce to the reader that you understand the significance of your findings for this area of scholarship. Moreover, you indicate what you would do differently or what new paths you would pursue to enhance the field's understanding of this debate and these sets of cases (or even related instances). By charting a hypothetical next course, you impress the reader with your enthusiasm and command of the discipline, and you help yourself for any future research paper assignments. Next time, you won't have to agonize about your research question. It will be set out for you in the Conclusion of your last paper!

For an example of a Conclusion, let's turn one last time to Diana's paper. Remember, she is trying to understand why the United States would attack Iraq but not North Korea, if it is determined to fight proliferation, particularly in rogue states. In this final section, Diana reminds the reader of the logics of her competing explanations, and then cites the evidence from her case studies that convinced her that one approach was stronger. She also carefully points out limitations in her study and begins a discussion of the broader implications of her findings for understanding other cases of American foreign policy. Diana has done a great job here. Note that the Conclusion is not simply one paragraph, that she recaps the highlights (conceptual and evidentiary) of the paper, recognizes some weaknesses, and considers the meaning of her findings for other cases. Perhaps she could have set out actual questions for future research or more boldly asserted the meaning of her findings for similar cases. What *exactly* does her research suggest about American decisions to intervene in Yugoslavia or Somalia? Why is the United States treating Iranian proliferation as it is? Still, Diana has done a fantastic job,[2] racing, not whimpering, to the finish line and turning in an excellent performance.

---

[2]You might fault Diana for not paying sufficient attention to the deterrent power of North Korea's military might and therefore not adequately assessing the Realist argument. That complaint is one for her Research Design (and it affects her ultimate judgment), but not one for the Conclusion where she is reporting her findings.

CONCLUSIONS AND BROADER IMPLICATIONS

United States foreign policy is a highly complex issue which is evaluated by numerous schools of thought. There may perhaps be no one theory that can account for the entire range of United States' international action, and different paradigms may apply to various time periods and case studies. During the Cold War, Realism's balance of power was the explanation which may have best fit the age and specific circumstances of U.S.-Soviet relations. In the post-Cold War era, however, the lines between enemy and ally are fuzzier, and thus new models must replace the old to explain the nature of American foreign policy and international affairs. Following the September 11th attacks on the World Trade Center and the Pentagon, the United States has embarked on a new era of international action which has been influenced by domestic opinions and a socially constructed perception of threat.

After evaluating the independent and dependent variables for both models, the Constructivist hypothesis proved to best fit the data available. The Realist argument failed in many respects to explain why the United States adopted a more aggressive policy towards Iraq, which seemingly posed less of a material threat than North Korea did. Both the size of the North Korean army and the amount of military expenditures were indicators to which a Realist would traditionally point to demonstrate that this East Asian state posed a high level of threat. American troops in this region also show North Korea's strategic military importance, not to mention the state's known WMD programs. Iraq, on the other hand, had a smaller military capability, spent less money on weapons, and far fewer U.S. troops were deployed in the region. As for Iraqi WMD programs, UN inspections failed to find the smoking gun of an Iraqi WMD program. North Korea posed the more imminent threat according to the Realist model, yet was dealt with diplomatically while the weaker Iraq was met with war. The Realist balance of power theory fails to explain this difference, and arguments of deterrence have little credence outside of the bipolar Cold War setting. In the present era of American hegemony, the Realist argument does not explain why the United States adopted opposite foreign policies towards Iraq and North Korea.

The Constructivist paradigm of socially constructed national interests does fit the data presented during the post-September 11th time period. Domestic perceptions of the international arena shape the foreign policy of a state which, according to Joseph Nye, is based in citizen deliberation and the democratic process.[3] The influence that global terrorism has had on U.S. foreign policy in the recent years can not be understated. September 11th was one of the most traumatic days in United States history, shaping citizens' ideas about their government and the world around them. Polling data showed the mentality of fear which was created following the attacks, and the societal propensity to favor retaliation for the September 11th atrocities. Domestic opinions were also shown to be more likely to favor a war with Iraq and a continued diplomacy with North Korea. Most citizens are not foreign policy experts, but rather are influenced by the highly publicized rhetoric of key public figures. This is true whether we look at FDR's fireside chats during the Great Depression and WW2, JFK's orations during the Cold War, or Bush's speeches since September 11th. The American public is easily influenced by an Administration's rhetoric, as is seen in the cases of Iraq and North Korea. President Bush and Secretary of State Colin Powell continually pressed the supposed links between September 11th, terrorism, and Iraq in practically all of their speeches in the months leading up to the Iraq war. Through the shrewd use of political speech, the Bush administration bent public understandings and opinions towards acceptance of war with Iraq and diplomatic relations with North Korea. American foreign policy toward Iraq and North Korea were thus influenced by citizens' perceptions of threat, which were bred in post-September 11th fears of terrorism and shaped by the Bush administration's rhetoric.

There are limitations to the findings of my research. First, I had a hard time finding data because Iraq and North Korea are rogue nations that provide little information about their activities, and open English-language sources on these countries are rather limited. If I had better information or unlimited time and resources to search for the figures, I could with more confidence confirm that the Realist hypothesis isn't

---

[3]Joseph S. Nye, Jr., *The Paradox of American Power: Why the World's Only Superpower Can't Go It Alone* (New York: Oxford University Press, 2002), p. 139.

upheld with the cases of North Korea and Iraq. Also, I would have liked to look at other similar cases of American interventions to see whether the Constructivist hypothesis would also hold. Finally, I would also have liked to have direct information about citizens' opinions immediately preceding and immediately after several important Bush administration speeches during the time period. Such poll data would allow me to further test how influential presidential rhetoric was on public opinion and the effects of public perceptions of threat on foreign policy.

Broader implications about the nature of U.S. foreign policy can be extrapolated from the cases of Iraq and North Korea. First, presidential rhetoric affected American citizens' understandings of key issues, which in turn influenced foreign policy. The Bush Administration's links between Iraq and terrorism helped to explain the discrepancy in intervention policy during the time period. To what extent have past public relations campaigns cleared the way for other interventions and international "police" actions? Second, the opinion of the American public was also shown to be of great importance to U.S. foreign policy considerations. Citizens were not impartial observers of world affairs and governmental policy, but rather were active participants who played important roles. Public opinion might help to explain why the United States goes to war or pulls out of other conflicts, like the ones in Yugoslavia and Somalia in the early 1990s. The Constructivist argument can thus be used to understand international politics in the modern age, and proves to be a compelling explanation of why the United States adopts the foreign policy it does.

PRACTICAL SUMMARY

Your Conclusion is an important part of your paper, so be sure to give it the attention that it deserves. It should accomplish five different tasks.

1. Tie the paper together by repeating the argument and reporting the findings.

2. Remind the reader why this argument is important to different audiences.

155

3. Assess the extent to which your thesis can be extended or must be limited.
4. Return to the choices or compromises that you made and evaluate their impact on your work.
5. Establish a productive path for future research.

SUGGESTED SCHEDULE

As the due date for your paper looms near (no less than a week before you need to turn it in), you should seek to finish writing your Conclusion. You need to complete the Conclusion early because even when this section is done, you still have some work to do. You need to revise and edit the paper. And you'll have an easier time with these tasks if you can put the paper down and clear your mind for a little while. So, follow the advice here and write your concluding section. You should now feel a great rush. You are almost done! You can see the finish line ahead!

9

Revising and Editing Your Work: Submitting with Pride a Polished Paper

I t's mile 25.[1] You are almost home. Your feet are hurting and your legs are aching, but you feel excited. You have now finished your draft, and you should do something to celebrate this accomplishment. As numerous authors have noted, writing a complete version of the paper is hard, and you should be very happy that you now have a whole draft. It is a great accomplishment, and if you celebrate and stop thinking about this work for a little while (preferably a day or at least several hours, not just a few minutes), you'll be in a better position to finish your research paper. Your mind should be fresh when you take on the tasks of revising and editing for the last time.

---

[1]I'm assuming that you've been revising and editing throughout the process as recommended in the book. If you have been writing straight through without reworking your text, the process discussed in this chapter will take much more attention. Having done no revising and editing, you are at the equivalent of mile 18 in the race. You can do it, but you've got to stay focused, and you need far more time to do the equivalent of running eight more miles.

Even if you've been revising as you go, the first completed full draft is seldom perfect. In fact, this version can often be quite awkward and problematic in places.[2] Therefore, you have a little more work to do (maybe another mile to run) before you can cross the finish line. Still, working with a complete draft—particularly one that has already been revised and edited in places—is much easier than starting from scratch. But you can always make it better. Because you have been pushed throughout this book to write often before you felt ready, you now have many pages of text to consider for their overall coherence and methodological soundness, as well as basic grammatical and usage problems. In other words, you need both to *revise* and *edit* your paper with the goal of producing a final draft of which you can feel enormously proud.

By now I hope that you have banished one of the most common misconceptions that many students have about writing. Most students believe that the world is divided into good writers and not-so-good writers. Some people are born knowing how to craft great sentences, paragraphs, and essays, and the rest of us are condemned to poor prose for the rest of our lives. This idea is nonsense! Writing, just like any talent—from sports to the arts, from cooking to calculus—is part inspiration but primarily skill. And you need to practice and hone skills to improve them. Thus, you should see your draft as a huge accomplishment because you have put your ideas on paper, but in subsequent iterations the paper will take on its polished shape. The vast majority of authors write their works in numerous drafts, and published authors in the social sciences produce many versions of their articles before the pieces actually land in a journal or with a publishing house. All authors, then, revise and edit before handing in a final draft.

Revising and *editing* are two distinct, though interrelated tasks. Revising entails making what we might call the "macro-level" changes to your text, any significant modifications in your ideas or the structure of your paper. Editing refers to the "micro-level" changes.

---

[2] Zerubavel, *The Clockwork Muse*, provides many quotes of famous authors who discuss the inadequacies of their first draft. Please note, however, that Zerubavel does not advocate revising carefully throughout the process as I have.

When you edit, you make sure that the text flows well and is grammatically correct, and that all your citations are provided and typed in the proper form, according to your professor's specifications. To submit a polished paper, you need to perform both of these tasks carefully. While you may view these jobs as tedious, think again about the metaphor of a race for your paper. Imagine if athletes could "re-run" their event to correct for mental and physical mistakes made or mishaps incurred. Revising and editing give you a chance to fix any of the problems that remain so that you can submit the best possible paper (or, metaphorically, run that great race). What a fantastic opportunity!

To revise effectively, you need to do several things. First, if you have previously handed in drafts, be sure to respond to everyone of your reader's suggestions. If you don't understand them, go talk to your instructor. If you disagree with them, also discuss this with your reader. If you are unable to have this discussion with your professor, explain your reasoning for rejecting the advice in a footnote. That way your reader can see that you took her comments seriously. The worst mistake you can make is to ignore the suggestions of someone who has read your work carefully (and who is going to grade it).

Second, go back to the Practical Summaries and the Writing Checklists at the end of this book's chapters as a way of double checking that each section accomplishes what it should. Third, make sure that the pieces of your paper fit together nicely. In other words, be sure that the transitions between sections work well, that introductions properly introduce and conclusions effectively conclude. Fourth, you will likely have new ideas about the significance of some information or concepts that you have developed during the writing process. You want to be sure that you integrate these new thoughts throughout the relevant parts of your paper. In other words, ensure that there is consistency throughout your work.

One section that you will certainly need to spend some time on is the Introduction. When you first wrote your draft of it you had not yet thought through the Research Design or performed the Analysis and Assessment. Now is the time to go back to be sure that the argument that you put forth is accurate and that the road map is complete and accurate. Also, take another look at your title. You shouldn't feel disappointed about either adjusting the Introduction or reconsidering the name of your paper. Imagine that three years ago you provided a friend a map to your house, and that person was to return today. If you failed to update your directions, the person might become lost, as exits on highways get renumbered (as do highways themselves), streets are renamed, and landmarks change or are eliminated. Think of the conceptual modifications that you have made over the course of writing your draft as "infrastructure improvements" to your paper.

In general, when you revise you will be changing, deleting, or adding major sections to your paper. While the first draft is an excellent beginning, do not be afraid to throw away or significantly change parts of the paper that no longer "work," that do not help you to achieve your goals or make your precise argument. For anyone, but especially for first-time authors, the idea of cutting or altering big sections of text is very painful. You feel that all the work you have done must "show" in explicit ways. Here again, remember the marathoner. We cannot see all of the 6- and 10-mile training runs that she did, nor the weightlifting, yet she would not be the runner she is without having trained her body in this manner. All we see is her race on the day of the marathon. A pared-down paper—with irrelevant sections cut—will demonstrate the quality that you desire. An experienced reader knows that a well-crafted text reflects a great understanding of the research process, your question, and your findings. So, do not be afraid to make changes and lose some of the work that you did before. You would not have arrived at your (higher) level of understanding of the problem if you had not written these now extraneous sections. Cut them, recognizing that this information was valuable to the process but is not needed for your paper any more.

In addition to making sure that the logic and structure of the paper are coherent and that every sentence and paragraph is essential to your overall argument, you want to pay close attention to micro-level issues. First and foremost, you should consult your syllabus and any special instructions that your professor has given you about this paper. Be sure that your final product conforms to all of the specifications. Second, be sure to *run the spell and grammar check program* that is standard on your word processor. As I am sure you know, these programs cannot find all problems—they sometimes identify specialized terms as misspellings or they may cause you some problems identifying "fragments" when you are trying to summarize qualitative information in a chart, but on balance, these programs are enormously useful, and I am amazed that more students haven't made a habit out of using them. The spell and grammar check will allow you to avoid silly errors (and may even teach you a bit about grammar, helping you to identify mistakes that you tend to make so that you can correct them in future writing, without the help of the program).

Third, you should take great care with your *word choice*, and there are three dimensions involved here. One goal throughout your paper is to express your ideas succinctly and precisely. You do not need to worry about using an impressive vocabulary, and you especially want to avoid using multi-syllable words that you can't define. You undermine your argument when you use language imprecisely and incorrectly. So, don't worry about including enough "big words." Instead, seek precision. Also make sure that you vary your language sufficiently throughout your paper. You might have found a great adjective, but if you use it five times in one paragraph the word becomes far less interesting and effective. Find another term—use a thesaurus or use the thesaurus function on your word processing program to help you.

Other problems with word choice come when, because of the topic or concept that you are researching, you need to write about a particular event or term many times. Here again, you need to come up with synonyms for this fundamentally important issue, occurrence, or idea, and should consult a thesaurus.

While you are thinking about word choice, use pronouns with great care. Not only should you limit their use, but you must make sure that the antecedent for any pronoun is clear and matches your term in number and gender. In addition, remember that "this" and "that" are indefinite pronouns that you might use to refer to complicated ideas or developments. The same rules apply to them. Find synonymous phrases for concepts or events and be sure the antecedent is clear and the pronoun appropriate.

As you edit your paper, you also want to pay close attention to your citations and any quotes or **paraphrases** that you have used. Make sure that your footnotes are complete and accurate. Be certain that you have included enough citations. Also check that your bibliography is in good shape. When looking at quotes, make sure that they are accurate and that the quotation marks are properly placed (unless you're using a long, indented quote, which does not require this form of punctuation). In American English, commas and periods go within the quotation marks, even if they are not the original author's. For paraphrases, go back and double check that the material is significantly different from the original text. Make sure you have not plagiarized. Also, whether paraphrasing or quoting, verify that you have included the correct page number or other identifying information for books, articles, sources from databases and websites so that an interested person could find your source if she wanted. In addition, confirm that your headings and your overall title accurately convey the meanings and purposes of the sections and the paper as a whole.

To be really happy with your paper and its flow, you would be well-served to get someone you respect and trust to read the paper, too. That person could see things that you might miss because you are, by now, so close to the text. If you do not have a friend that you would like as a reader, consider taking it over to your institution's "Writing Center" to get a fresh pair of trained eyes to give you advice. You can also read your paper out loud. That advice might seem funny and sound painful—oh no, I have to listen to my own words! To listen carefully to the sound is precisely the point—you want to rely on your ears now, to help you find any problems that your eyes may have overlooked. Your ears will tell you what sounds "funny," and you should make the necessary adjustments on the basis of what the text "sounds" like.

Some of you may think that your ears are unreliable, and maybe you are right. But please realize that you can improve your use of language (maybe not today, but over the next few months and years) if you pay attention to it. To improve your ability to identify good usage, I suggest that you read—fiction or nonfiction books, newspapers, magazines, and anything that you find interesting. Make a habit of reading for pleasure every day, even if only for 15 minutes. Surely, you can find that time! And when you read, pay attention to the language, don't just zoom across the page. You might even consider reading some things out loud so that you can hear what good, clear writing sounds like. Then, start to be aware of how you talk and how you can communicate verbally in a clearer and more effective manner. You will be amazed at how much you can change your mode of expression if you put your mind to it.

Before handing in the paper, you may also want to consult one of the many pocket style manuals to help you with problems that you may have with punctuation or *homonym confusion*.[3] If you learn the rules of punctuation, or become familiar with any words that are giving you trouble, you should be able to "cure" this difficulty for the future. Also, you should try to transform *passive constructions*—places in the text where the subject is not performing the action of the verb— into active ones. Again, a good style manual can help you both identify and change these. Generally, English speakers consider active constructions to be clearer and better style than passive ones.

One last piece of micro-level advice: Avoid using *colloquialisms*, and personal pronouns, especially the second person (either plural or singular) pronoun "you" in formal writing. I know that I have violated this rule throughout this book; I have purposely written it in a conversational style. Your research paper, however, is to be written in a formal style, like a journal article or a scholarly book. Thus, you neither want to use colloquialisms (unless you are quoting an important source directly) nor have a conversation with the reader.

Now you are ready to print your paper. Before doing so, run the spell and grammar check again. Then, read over the text one last time (You probably have made additional changes; even after the machine has confirmed that the paper is fine, sometimes in making small corrections you can introduce some silly errors.) Confirm that you have included page numbers in your text. Then, view each printed page on your screen. If you need to, change the page breaks so charts, graphs,

---

[3]One of my favorites is Diana Hacker, *A Pocket Style Manual*, 4th ed. (Boston, MA: Bedford/St. Martin's Books, 2004).

or tables fit fully on one (unless they are too long) and headings are not left **"widowed"** or **"orphaned"** from their sections. (In other words, you want to be sure that one line from a paragraph or table is not found on one page while the rest is on another.) Now you are finally ready to print. After printing, verify that the pages are in the proper order, and staple (or some professors prefer paper clips) your paper in the top left corner. (You have double-checked all the relevant instructions, so you know how to present this paper to please your professor.) *Et Voila!* You are finally done. Congratulations on a polished research paper in Political Science. You have done it, and now, celebrate your accomplishment!

PRACTICAL SUMMARY

After you have finished your first draft you have completed the bulk of your work, but you still are not done. You need to revise and edit. To accomplish these tasks, I suggest that you do the following:

To Revise

1. Respond to every comment that your reader made. If you don't understand or disagree with some of them, discuss your questions with your instructor.
2. Treat each section of your paper as a stand-alone essay. Go back and read the "Practical Summary" from the relevant chapter in this book to determine what the goals were for that section. Then read that part of your research paper, making any changes necessary so that your section accomplishes all that it should.
3. After you are satisfied that each piece of the paper is in excellent shape, make sure that the transitions between sections are good. Be sure that the parts logically flow into each other, titles and subtitles are adequate, and introductory and concluding paragraphs do their jobs well.
4. Verify that any new ideas that you developed as you proceeded with your paper are effectively integrated throughout. For instance, you will likely have to spend a good deal of time modifying your introduction so that it adequately reflects your finished draft. Do not be afraid to make necessary deletions and additions of text.

To Edit

1. Run the spell and grammar check function on your computer. Make the changes recommended if they make sense to you. Assume that the program is right, but remember, the program can find problems that might not actually be mistakes, such as special terms that it identifies as misspellings or fragments that are purposely included in your text.

2. Pay close attention to word choice. Make sure that your language is precise (e.g., get rid of "big words" that you cannot define), avoid using the same word or term over and over again, and watch out for overusing pronouns.

3. Make sure your citations (both within the text and at the end of the paper) are complete and accurate. Take great care that any quotes or paraphrases are correctly included.

4. Double-check your syllabus and any assignment sheets to make sure that you have abided by any special instructions that your professor has given you.

5. Check the overall quality of your paper by consulting an outside reader and/or by reading it out loud. Change the text if it doesn't "sound good."

6. Fix other grammar or usage mistakes such as punctuation, homonym confusion, passive constructions, colloquialisms, and the use of second-person pronouns.

7. Run spell and grammar check again. Make necessary changes.

8. Read again. Correct any remaining errors.

9. Before printing, look at how the printed pages will appear. Make sure that you have included numbers on each page. Adjust page breaks to keep key parts of the text together on the same page.

10. Print your paper, and staple or paper clip it (depending on your professor's instructions), being sure that the pages are in the proper order.

11. You are done. Celebrate and feel proud!

SUGGESTED SCHEDULE

In the last week or several days (notice that I *did not say* the last night or hours) before the paper is due, you must finish the tasks of editing and revising. In general, after you think you have finished your final draft, you should put your paper down for a day or at least several hours to give yourself perspective. Follow the steps spelled out here and you will be in fine shape. Then, you can more effectively revise and edit your work. When you are satisfied, print out your paper. Hooray! You've written a high-quality research paper. What a great accomplishment!

CHECKLIST FOR FINAL DRAFT

Below is a checklist to consult while you are writing the fourth and final installment of your research paper. Fill it out accurately, and any time you cannot check off an item, you need to go back and address the problem. If you have proceeded as recommended, at this point you are writing a first draft of your Conclusion, and revising everything that came before based on the earlier comments you have received or ideas that have emerged as you have continued working on the project. As before, the checklist identifies all the key elements of this new section and indicates that you should have gone back and tackled any problems that you or your professor identified with earlier sections of your paper. Again, you can see that writing issues figure prominently here.

Writing the Conclusion

1. Does your conclusion tie the paper together for the reader by reminding her of the thesis and where the weight of the evidence fell? _____

2. Does your conclusion explain why your argument and findings are important and interesting to different audiences (scholars, policy makers, and citizens)? _____

3. Does your conclusion consider whether you can apply your findings to other cases (from other time periods, to other countries, to other individuals)? If you can extend your findings, do you say what your findings would mean for other prominent cases today? _____

4. Does your conclusion consider whether the choices you made in your Research Design (operationalizing and selecting cases) had an effect on your findings?

If you had frustrating results, do you discuss how to operationalize or select cases differently? _____

5. Does your conclusion discuss what would be fruitful avenues for future research? _____

Revisions

6. Have you responded to all the previous comments on your earlier papers? _____

7. Have you developed smooth transitions between sections of your paper? _____

8. Have you given the sections of your paper interesting and appropriate titles? _____

9. Did you make sure that your Introduction makes a good impression on the reader by presenting your puzzle and research question, explaining why it is interesting and important to various audiences, and providing a road map? _____

10. Have you made sure that any new ideas have been worked through the whole draft? _____

Editing

11. Have you checked for the usage problems that generally cause you difficulties? _____

12. Have you checked for how the paper will look before you print it, being sure that no section headings are left orphaned or widowed? _____

13. Have you looked at all the information and special instructions that your professor has given you for this paper (number of pages, precise format, any extra information about the title page, etc.) and abided by them? _____

Writing and Format Concerns

14. Have you properly cited the sources of your ideas? Have you avoided plagiarism? Do all your citations conform to the appropriate format? _____

15. Have you avoided long quotes? _____

16. Have you run the spell and grammar check, recognizing that this function does not catch all errors? _____

17. Have you numbered your pages, but not the title page? _____

18. Have you included a bibliography that conforms to the format specified? _____

19. Recognizing the limits of spell and grammar check, have you edited your paper? _____

20. Add your own personal writing concerns (by now you should have a very specific personal list).
    - split infinitives _____
    - sentence fragments _____
    - run-on sentences _____
    - good transitions _____
    - word choice/overuse of words _____
    - homonym confusion _____
    - overuse of pronouns _____
    - passive voice _____
    - length of paragraphs (more than a sentence, less than a page) _____
    - other _____ _____
    - other _____ _____

Glossary

Academic Search Premier an online database excellent for searching for information from scholarly journals, newsmagazines, and newspapers.

American Politics a subfield in the discipline of Political Science, where the focus is the U.S. government and the American political process.

Analysis and Assessment a section of your research paper, also called the "Data Analysis" or "Case Study Section." In this part of the paper, you evaluate your hypothesis or thesis based on the plan that you have established for yourself in your Research Design. You "tell the story" of the relationship between the variables or key factors in your argument in this section.

argument also called a thesis or hypothesis. This is your best-guess answer in response to your research question. In your paper, you determine whether you can sustain your argument based on logic, normative claims (for nor-mative papers), and evidence (empirical research).

best guess your hypothesis, which is your best, educated guess as to the answer to your research question.

case one incident of the phenomenon that you are studying. If you're interested in voting behavior, for instance, you could conceive of each voter as a case.

case study in qualitative research, an in-depth analysis of one particular incident. For instance, if you were studying the causes of intervention in the post-Cold War era, one case study would be an analysis of the American intervention in Haiti. Case studies may be part of the Analysis and Assessment portion of the paper, and the hypothesis always guides them.

causation (causal relationship) an instance when at least one factor (cause) brings about an effect. Adjustments in one factor necessarily occur *with* changes in the other.

Comparative Politics one of the sub-fields in Political Science, in which students examine why politics is the way it is in different states around the world. The focus here is on using the comparative method and developing general understandings of political institutions, processes, and cultures as well as appreciating the differences between regions and polities.

Conclusion the last section of your research paper. It accomplishes five tasks: reminds the reader of the thesis and where the weight of the evidence came down; discusses why the argument and the particular findings are important and what they mean to various audiences; assesses the versatility and limits of your thesis; critically evaluates your accomplishments; and serves as a jumping-off point for future research.

Constructivism an interpretivist perspective in International Relations that would fit under the generic Culturalist paradigm in Political Science. It stresses that structures are social as well as material, and that meanings are constructed through interactions, knowledge, and resources.

content analysis a form of data analysis in which the researcher evaluates texts to determine the numerical incidences of (quantitative) or the general disposition toward (qualitative) particular words, phrases, or themes.

continuous variable a variable that will hold values that range along a continuum. It can also be referred to as *interval*.

control the attempt to minimize the impact of other factors on your study. In selecting cases, you try to hold other factors constant to eliminate or reduce the possible effects of other variables on your subject.

correlation instances when two or more factors change together. Adjustments in one factor necessarily occur *with* changes in the other, but changes in one factor do not necessarily cause changes in the other.

Culturalism one of the four generic schools of thought in Political Science. Culturalists contend that there are sets of rules and norms embedded in society that govern and guide an actor's behavior. These conventions can be at the level of a national, regional, or local culture. Please note that among culturalists there can be great debate. Some argue culture is constructed, believing that it is malleable and, often, that elites can manipulate it for their own purposes, while others contend that culture is primordial, i.e. original and unchanging.

data information to be used to evaluate your argument, thesis, or hypothesis. Data can be either qualitative or quantitative.

database an online resource of information. Often this consists of multiple years of many journals, newspapers, or other media sources. It can also consist of information collected by a particular organization, such as the UN Human Development statistics. Typically, you must access this information through a library; it is not available freely on the internet.

degrees of freedom for a Chi-Square analysis, a number that you need to calculate in order to determine whether your hypothesis is confirmed or not. The formula for it is (rows−1) × (columns−1).

dependent variable the effect or phenomenon under investigation. It "depends" on some other factors (the causes or independent variables). It is a variable because, depending on what value the cause takes on, the effect will change.

dummy variable in regression analysis, a variable that measures the presence or absence of a characteristic. For instance, we might be looking at female/or not (i.e. male), caucasian/or not, Catholic/or not.

Economic Determinists adherents of economism or economic determinism.

Economism/Economic Determinism one of the four generic schools of thought in Political Science. Its adherents contend that economic conditions drive politics.

editing the process of fixing grammatical, punctuation, or word choice errors.

empirical observable, the part of a research paper that examines the evidence. Within the discipline, there are two kinds of empirical research, theory-based research and public policy analysis.

evidence data or information relevant to your thesis, which helps you determine the extent to which the argument is sustainable.

fragment an incomplete sentence.

Google an extremely powerful search engine for the internet. While most students immediately think that they should "Google" a topic when they want information on it, in this book you learn that you often should check databases for scholarly information first. For all kinds of information, you should always use the internet with care, picking only sites whose veracity you can trust.

grammar check a word processing function that will find grammatical errors.

headings the titles for your sections of your paper. Research papers should be written in sections and each of the sections should have headings. Headings are not a substitute for a transition, but they mark a change in emphasis. In Chicago style, major headings are centered on the page and written in all capital letters, while the first level sub-headings are left-justified and underlined.

hypothesis your best guess for the answer to your research question. Often synonymous with argument and thesis in common usage. In an empirical paper the hypothesis takes the form "The more of X (independent variable), the more of Y (dependent variable)" for a positive relationship of continuous variables; or "If X is A, then Y is B, but if X is C, then Y is D," for a category variable.

independent variable the cause of the effect or phenomenon under investigation; changes in the independent variable necessarily cause changes in the effect or dependent variable.

indicators in transforming a concept into a variable (operationalizing), indicators are the factors that you will look at to come up with the value of your variable. In our example in the text, the power of a state was a function of three indicators: (a) the size of its armed forces, (b) the level of defense spending, and (c) the number of nonconventional weapons (nuclear, biological, chemical, radiological) in its arsenal.

Institutionalism one of the four generic schools of thought in Political Science. Its adherents contend that institutions exert primary causal power in politics. Institutions provide incentives that encourage some behaviors and discourage others. Thus, they define for all (e.g. citizens, elites, groups, or states, depending on one's subfield) how to win rewards and receive punishments in the system, thereby affecting the players' actions.

International Relations a subfield in Political Science (sometimes also called International Politics). It examines the interactions and external behaviors of states, international organizations, and other international nongovernmental organizations, as well as the norms and identities that develop among these actors over time.

interpretivism an approach in Political Science, usually contrasted with rationalism. It assumes that actors construct their identities and interests on the basis of their past and present interactions with others in a system.

interval data one of three different types of data. Interval data is information that can be expressed in numeric form (e.g., spending, dollars, votes, etc). If both your independent and dependent variables can be measured with interval data, then you should use regression analysis to evaluate your hypothesis.

Introduction   the first section of your research paper. It is a very important section because it makes that vital first impression on your reader. It is a type of contract between you and the reader, establishing the parameters of your work. In general, introductions begin by stating your specific research question (preferably not in question form), continue by explaining why this question is interesting and important to different audiences (political scientists, policy makers, and citizens), and provide a road map to the rest of the paper, introducing the reader very briefly to your schools of thought, your argument, your cases, and your findings.

journal of opinion   a magazine that has a clear ideological leaning. Excellent ones include, among others, *The Weekly Standard* (conservative) and *The American Prospect* (liberal/progressive). These sources are excellent places to find controversial issues for study.

Journal Storage: The Scholarly Archive (JSTOR)   an online database that you can search to find articles from the premier journals in the social sciences, humanities, and natural sciences.

Lexis–Nexis   an online database for searching legal sources (Lexis) and news sources (Nexis) from around the world.

literature   for academics, this term means the key articles and books on a particular topic.

Literature Review   the second section of your paper, following the Introduction. The Literature Review is an analysis of the scholarly debate on your research question in its most general, concise form. The Literature Review uncovers the multiple answers that scholars studying the same general question have given and groups these answers into schools of thought. In this section, you give each school a label, which can be standards in the field or specific, new ones that you have developed.

measurement strategy   also called operationalization. It is your plan for transforming the concepts that you have identified in your hypothesis into knowable entities.

methodology   the approaches that you are going to use to evaluate your hypothesis, all spelled out in your Research Design section.

model   a pictorial representation of the variables in the most-preferred school of thought that was identified in the Literature Review, typically presented in the X (independent variable) → Y (dependent variable) form. In empirical papers, it is found in the Model and Hypothesis section.

model and hypothesis   a brief, but important section of an empirical paper, coming after the Literature Review. In it, you clearly identify the independent and dependent variables and present them in X → Y form (model). While the model helps you zero in on the cause and effect, the hypothesis explains precisely how the variables are linked to each other. The hypothesis is written in sentence form, usually of the structure, "The more of X, the more of Y" (for positive relationships of continuous variables) or "If X is A, then Y is B" (for category variables).

negative relationship   occurs if the increase in the causal factor (independent variable) leads to a decrease in the effect (dependent variable). If the relationship were charted, the curve would be downward sloping and therefore the slope would be some negative number.

nonempirical   not relying on data or facts, but rather on equations, logic, or values.

normative explicitly concerned with values and what ought or should be. The subfield of Political Theory is normative. In political science, research can be either normative or empirical.

observed values the information that you collected or observed. This terminology is typically used in quantitative analysis.

operationalize the process of transforming the concepts that you have identified in your hypothesis into knowable entities (variables). Also called a measurement strategy. You accomplish this important task in your Research Design.

ordinal measure information that comes in category form, but the categories can be rank ordered on some criteria (for instance, along an ideological spectrum). You cannot, however, specify the exact distance between the categories. (If you could specify that distance, then this information would be interval, not ordinal.)

orphans bits of text (for instance, the first line of a paragraph or a chart) that appear as a single line at the bottom of a page. Before turning in a final draft, all "orphans" should be united with at least part of the "family" by moving the page break.

page breaks at the end of a typed page, where the text stops. Sometimes, when including charts, graphs, or new section headings, you may have to force a page break so that these graphics or headings and texts can appear together.

paraphrase to rewrite the sense of another author's text. Paraphrases are always footnoted, but they are significantly different from the original text. In order to paraphrase appropriately, you typically have to close the book and work to distill the sense of a much larger text into a smaller one.

parsimony the state of having fewer explanatory factors (independent variables).

passive construction a type of sentence structure in which the subject is not performing the action of the verb. Typical passive constructions include "It was Pakistan that was the first Muslim country to develop a nuclear bomb" or "Nuclear weapons in the Muslim world were first developed by Pakistan." The preferred construction is called **active,** and active voice communicates those same ideas as "Pakistan was the first Muslim state to develop nuclear weapons."

peer review the policy of having peers read and evaluate a text. With respect to journals, peer-review ones send out any piece that comes in for consideration to other experts to review and approve. This is the type of source you need to consult for a literature review.

Political Theory the subfield in Political Science that examines the foundations of politics and political ideas, typically by examining the works of key political philosophers. Sometimes this body of work is called "the canon." Political Theorists engage in normative research. This subfield is also referred to as Political Thought or Political Philosophy.

political theory research normative research in which the inquiry typically starts with the key words what ought or should. Political Theory research also delves into the meaning of key ideas in politics by looking at the works of important philosophers and evaluating their logic.

positive relationship occurs between two variables if the increase in the causal factor (independent variable) would lead to an increase in the effect (dependent variable). If the relationship were charted, the curve would be upward sloping and therefore the slope would be some positive number.

Power Approach one of the generic schools of thought within Political Science. The Power school asserts that actors are rational and respond primarily to the structure of power. Thus, if an actor is weak, it will seek out others to protect itself and create a balance, or if an actor is strong, it may inspire fear in others and be able to control outcomes. In International Politics, this school follows from the intellectual tradition called Realism. This can also be classified as a Rational Choice or Materialist perspective.

primary source a source of information that is relatively "unprocessed," that is uninterpreted by a scholar. Plans for operationalizing your concepts using primary source materials are most impressive, as you are doing original empirical research.

prove to show something to be true. In the social sciences, we are not seeking to prove our hypotheses, but to evaluate whether they hold true in certain instances or not. If you're interested in proofs, become a mathematician!

proxy variable a variable that will stand in for another. At times we can't actually calculate our desired concept, like the probability of war, so we develop a suitable substitute (proxy) for it.

public policy research investigations of contemporary problems and their solutions to see what can be done to fix them and how well solutions are working. This is a form of empirical research.

puzzle in Political Science, an intellectual dilemma typically regarding an event or development that either lacks obvious answers or where the obvious answers appear to be incorrect. Puzzles are excellent inspirations for a research question and, if you've found one, your puzzle should figure prominently in your paper's Introduction.

ProQuest an online database, excellent for searching for information from scholarly journals, newsmagazines, and newspapers.

qualitative analysis a form of analysis in which the evidence is in the form of words.

quantitative analysis a form of analysis in which the evidence is numeric and the ultimate assessment dependents on statistics and measures.

reify to think of an abstract concept as real. When operationalizing concepts and coming up with quantitative measures, be sure to avoid reifying. For example, the balance of power is a concept that is useful in political science, but it is not an existing reality.

report a traditional paper (i.e., one that you would write prior to reading this book) in which you describe everything you can find out about a political phenomenon or process. Your report is typically organized by chronology. In this book, a report contrasts with a research paper, and after learning how to write a research paper, you will never write a report for your Political Science classes again!

Rationalism a perspective in the social sciences which assumes that actors are rational and identities and interests are formed prior to (or not dependent upon) interactions with others in the system; usually contrasted with interpretivism.

Research Design the section in the research paper that follows the Model and Hypothesis, in which you present your plan for carrying out your research and your justification for this approach. Typically, it consists of four subsections: operationalizing of concepts, selecting cases, identifying sources, and methods for generating information (surveys, questionnaires, etc.).

research question the specific question that your paper seeks to answer. For empirical papers, it usually begins with "Why," "How," "To what extent," or "Under what conditions" and for normative ones it usually starts with "Ought," "Should," "What ought," "How should," or "What would theorist X say about."

revising   the process of making macro-level changes to your text so that each section of the paper accomplishes its necessary tasks and the logic is consistent throughout. At times, revising requires changing, deleting, moving, or adding major ideas and sections to your paper.

road map   a part of your Introduction, it is a basic sketch or outline of your whole paper written in paragraph or sentence form. In the road map, you provide a sentence or two summary of each of the other sections of the paper (Literature Review, Model and Hypothesis, Research Design, Analysis and Assessment, and Conclusion).

sample   a subset of the universe of cases. You must choose your sample very carefully in order to minimize bias.

scatterplot   a graphing of the data, with the independent variable along the *x*-axis and the dependent variable along the *y*-axis.

scholar   professors (working at universities or colleges) or people employed by think tanks, public policy institutes, and governmental institutes. These people tend to publish their work in what are called peer-review journals, periodicals with a policy of sending out any piece that comes in for con-sideration to other experts to review and approve.

scholarly source   a source in which scholars publish, such as peer-review journals or books published by university presses or other publishing houses that use other academic experts to review works before deciding to publish them.

school of thought   in your literature review, a scholarly answer to the general research question that you identify. These answers typically posit a different causal variable to account for the same effect (dependent variable). Each school of thought should have a label and at least one academic associated with it.

secondary source   a source of information that has been "processed," that is, interpreted by someone else. Be careful in using secondary sources in your Analysis and Assessment section because some other student of your research question (the author of your source) has already interpreted the data to reach his conclusion.

spell check   a word processing function that will find spelling errors.

subfield   an area of inquiry in an academic discipline. In American Political Science, there are at least six: American Politics, Political Theory, Comparative Politics, International Relations, Public Policy, and Methodology.

test a hypothesis   to determine whether the data are consistent with your best guess. This is the purpose of the Analysis and Assessment section of your paper. Please note: Your goal is NOT to prove your hypothesis, but to evaluate it. You are not an advocate for your hypothesis.

theory-oriented research   a term coined by W. Phillips Shively to describe empirical research that is basic in nature, that is, it seeks to uncover truths about politics instead of solving a practical problem.

thesis   a contentious statement, that is, a declaration or description with which reasonable people could disagree. A thesis can be either a normative claim or an empirically verifiable contention. Often used as a synonym for argument or hypothesis.

title   the name of your paper and another important way (along with your Intro-duction) to make an excellent first impression. Good titles communicate your research question or puzzle, cases, and findings in a provocative, evocative, alliterative, or otherwise appealing way.

thesaurus a reference book (or word processing function) that allows you to find synonyms and antonyms, especially useful in varying word choice, so that you are not constantly using the same word or phrase. Have your thesaurus handy in the editing stage.

topic an area of inquiry that typically can be described. In writing a research paper, you need to transform your topic into a research question so that you can explain or illustrate an argument.

universe of cases all the possible events of the phenomenon under study. For instance, if you were studying American presidential elections, the universe of cases would be all the elections for president from George Washington's first election to the present.

variable anything that can vary, that is, change in value.

widows bits of text (for instance, a heading or the first line of a paragraph or a chart) that appear on the subsequent page. Before turning in a final draft, all "widows" should be brought back with at least part of the "family" (its section or text) by moving the page break.

word choice the language that you use. In editing, readers may note "word choice" problems, which typically mean that you have used improper language or you are over-using certain terms.

Bibliography

Baglione, Lisa A. *To Agree or Not to Agree: Leadership, Bargaining, and Arms Control*. Ann Arbor: University of Michigan Press, 1999.

Best, Judith A. *The Choice of the People? Debating the Electoral College*. Lanham, MD: Rowman & Littlefield Publishers, 1996.

Bickel, Alexander. *Reform and Continuity: The Electoral College, the Convention, and the Party System*. New York: Harper & Row, 1971.

Bowen, John R. "The Myth of Global Ethnic Conflict." *Journal of Democracy* 7, no. 4 (1996): 3–14.

Boyd, Richard. "Thomas Hobbes and the Perils of Pluralism." *The Journal of Politics* 63 (2001): 392–413.

Calhoun, John C. "A Disquisition of Government." In *American Political Thought*, 5th ed., edited by Kenneth M. Dolbeare and Michael S. Cummings, 212–224. Washington, DC: Congressional Quarterly Press, 2004.

Campbell, Donald T. and Julian C. Stanley. *Experimental and Quasi-Experimental Designs for Research*. Boston: Houghton Mifflin, 1963.

Castle, Michelle. "'You Can't Always Get What You Want, But If You Try, You Get What You Need': The Confirmation Process of Justices of the Supreme Court." Senior Honors Thesis, Saint Joseph's University, 2005.

Chilcote, Ronald H. *Theories of Comparative Politics: The Search for a Paradigm Reconsidered*, 2nd ed. Boulder: Westview Press, 1994.

Clarke, Simon, Peter Fairbrother, Michael Burawoy, and Pavel Krotov. *What about the Workers? Workers and the Transition to Capitalism in Russia*. New York: Verso, 1993.

Dahl, Robert. *How Democratic is the American Constitution?* New Haven: Yale University Press, 2002.

Deans, Thomas. *Writing and Community Action: A Service-Learning Rhetoric with Readings*. New York: Longman, 2003.

Gaddis, John Lewis. *We Now Know: Rethinking Cold War History*. New York: Oxford University Press, 1997.

George, Alexander L. and Andrew Bennett, *Case Studies and Theory Development in the Social Sciences*. Cambridge: MIT Press, 2004.

Hacker, Diana. *A Pocket Manual of Style,* 4th ed. Boston: Bedford/St. Martin's, 2004.

Hamilton, Alexander, James Madison, and John Jay. *The Federalist Papers.* Edited by Clinton Rossiter. New York: The New American Library of World Literature, 1961.

Huntington, Samuel P. "The Clash of Civilizations?" *Foreign Affairs* 72, no. 3 (1993): 22–49.

_____. *Who Are We? The Challenges to America's National Identity.* New York: Simon & Schuster, 2004.

Ishiyama, John. "Examining the Impact of the Wahlke Report: Surveying the Structure of the Political Science Curricula at Liberal Arts and Sciences Colleges and Universities in the Midwest." *PS: Political Science and Politics* 38, no. 1 (2005): 71–74.

Johnson, Janet Buttolph and Richard A. Joslyn. *Political Science Research Methods,* 3rd ed. Washington, DC: Congressional Quarterly Press, 1995.

_____. *Political Science Research Methods*, 5th ed. Washington, DC: Congressional Quarterly Press, 2005.

Katznelson, Ira and Helen V. Milner, eds. *Political Science: State of the Discipline,* Centennial Edition. New York: W.W. Norton, 2005.

Kegley Jr., Charles W. and Eugene R. Wittkopf. *World Politics: Trend and Transformation,* 9th ed. Belmont, CA: Wadsworth/Thomson Learning, 2004.

Keohane, Robert. *After Hegemony: Cooperation and Discord in the World Political Economy.* Princeton: Princeton University Press, 1984.

Keohane, Robert O. and Lisa L. Martin. "The Promise of Institutionalist Theory." *International Security* 20 (1995): 39–51.

Krasner, Stephen D. *Defending the National Interest: Raw Materials Investment and U.S. Foreign Policy.* Princeton: Princeton University Press, 1978.

_____, ed. *International Regimes.* Ithaca: Cornell University Press, 1983.

Kurland, Philip B. and Ralph Lerner, eds. *The Founders' Constitution,* vol. 3. Chicago: University of Chicago Press, 1987.

Lijphart, Arend. "Comparative Politics and the Comparative Method." *American Political Science Review* 65 (1971): 682–693.

_____. "How the Cases You Choose Determine the Answers You Get." *Journal of Policy Analysis* 2 (1975): 131–152.

Lipset, Seymour Martin. *Political Man: The Social Bases of Politics*. Baltimore: Johns Hopkins University Press, 1981.

Linz, Juan J. and Arturo Valenzuela, eds. *The Limits of Presidential Democracy.* Vol. 1. Baltimore: Johns Hopkins University Press, 1994.

Linz, Juan J. "The Perils of Presidentialism." *Journal of Democracy* 1, no. 1 (1990): 51–69.

Lowi, Theodore J. "American Business, Public Policy, Case Studies and Political Theory." *World Politics* 16 (1964): 677–715.

_____. *The End of Liberalism: The Second Republic of the United States,* 2nd ed. New York: W.W. Norton, 1979.

_____. *The Personal President: Power Invested, Promise Unfulfilled.* Ithaca, NY: Cornell University Press, 1985.

Magstadt, Thomas M. *Nations and Governments: Comparative Politics in Regional Perspective,* 5th ed. Belmont, CA: Wadsworth/Thomson Learning, 2005.

McCann, Michael. *Rights at Work: Pay Equity and the Politics of Legal Mobilization.* Chicago: University of Chicago Press, 1994.

McDonald, Forrest. *E Pluribus Unum: The Formation of the American Republic 1776–1790.* Boston: Houghton Mifflin Company, 1965.

McGovern, Stephen J. *The Politics of Downtown Development: Dynamic Political Cultures in San Francisco and Washington, DC.* Lexington, KY: University Press of Kentucky, 1999.

Mearsheimer, John J. "Back to the Future: Instability in Europe after the Cold War." *International Security* 15 (1990): 5–56.

Midlarsky, Manus, ed. *Handbook of War Studies II.* Ann Arbor: University of Michigan Press, 2000.

Morgenthau, Hans and Kenneth W. Thompson, *Politics among Nations: The Struggle for Power and Peace,* 6th ed. New York: Alfred A. Knopf, 1985.

Mughan, Anthony. Review of *Presidentialism, Parliamentarism and Stable Democracy: The Failure of Presidential Democracy,* by Juan J. Linz and Arturo Valenzuela. *Mershon International Studies Review* 39 (1995): 123–125.

Neuman, W. Lawrence. *Social Research Methods: Qualitative and Quantitative Approaches,* 5th ed. New York: Allyn and Bacon, 2003.

Nincic, Miroslav. "U.S. Soviet Policy and the Electoral Connection." *World Politics* 42 (1990): 370–96.

Norris, Pippa and Ronald Inglehart. "Cultural Obstacles to Equal Representation." *Journal of Democracy* 12, no. 3 (2001): 126–140.

Nye, Jr., Joseph S. *The Paradox of American Power: Why the World's Only Superpower Can't Go It Alone.* New York: Oxford University Press, 2002.

Przeworski, Adam and Fernando Limongi Neto, "Modernization: Theories and Facts." *World Politics* 49 (1997): 155–183.

Putnam, Robert D. *Bowling Alone: The Collapse and Revival of American Community.* New York: Simon & Schuster, 2000.

_____. with Robert Leonardi and Raffaella Y. Nanetti, *Making Democracy Work: Civic Traditions in Modern Italy.* Princeton, NJ: Princeton University Press, 1993.

Rabinow, Paul and William M. Sullivan, eds. *Interpretive Social Science: A Reader.* Berkeley: University of California Press, 1979.

Rosenberg, Gerald. *The Hollow Hope: Can Courts Bring About Social Change?* Chicago: University of Chicago Press, 1991.

Rostow, Walt W. *Stages of Economic Growth: A Non-Communist Manifesto.* New York: Cambridge University Press, 1960.

Shively, W. Phillips. *The Craft of Political Research,* 5th ed. Upper Saddle Brook, NJ: Prentice Hall, 2002.

Sidlow, Edward and Beth Henschen, *America at Odds,* 4th ed. Belmont, CA: Wadsworth/Thomson Learning, 2004.

Singer, J. David. "The Level-of-Analysis Problem in International Relations." In *The International System: Theoretical Essays,* edited by J. David Singer, Klaus Knorr, and Sidney Verba. Princeton: Princeton University Press, 1961.

Stone, Clarence N. *Regime Politics: Governing of Atlanta, 1946–1988.* Lawrence: University Press of Kansas, 1989.

Taylor, Charles. "Interpretation and the Sciences of Man." In *Interpretive Social Science: A Reader,* edited by Paul Rabinow and William M. Sullivan. Berkeley: University of California Press, 1979, 25–71.

Vasquez, John A. and Marie T. Henehan. *The Scientific Study of Peace and War: A Text Reader.* Lanham, MD: Lexington Books, 1999.

Wahlke, John C. "Liberal Learning and the Political Science Major: A Report to the Profession." *PS: Political Science and Politics* 24 (1991): 48–60.

Wallerstein, Immanuel. *The Capitalist World Economy: Essays.* New York: Cambridge University Press, 1979.

Waltz, Kenneth N. *Man, the State, and War: A Theoretical Analysis.* New York: Columbia University Press, 1959.

_____. "Origins of War in Neorealist Theory." *Journal of Interdisciplinary History* 18, no. 4 (1988): 39–52.

Welch, Susan, John Gruhl, John Comer, and Susan M. Rigdon. *American Government,* 9th ed. Belmont, CA: Wadsworth/Thomson Learning, 2004.

Wendt, Alexander. "Anarchy Is What States Make of It: The Social Construction of Power Politics." *International Organization* 46 (1992): 391–425.

_____. "Constructing International Politics," *International Security* 20 (1995): 71–81.

Zeidenstein, Harvey. *Direct Election of the President.* Lexington, MA: Lexington Books, 1973.

Zerubavel, Eviatar. *The Clockwork Muse: A Practical Guide to Writing Theses, Dissertations, and Books.* Cambridge, MA: Harvard University Press, 1999.

Index